INFORMATION LITERACY ASSESSMENT

Standards-Based Tools and Assignments

Teresa Y. Neely

Foreword by
Hannelore Rader

AMERICAN LIBRARY ASSOCIATION
Chicago   2006

Composition by ALA Editions using QuarkXpress 5.0 on a PC platform. Typefaces: New Caledonia and Helvetica Narrow.

Printed on 50-pound white offset, a pH-neutral stock, and bound in 10-point cover stock by Batson Printing.

The paper used in this publication meets the minimum requirements of American National Standard for Information Sciences—Permanence of Paper for Printed Library Materials, ANSI Z39.48-1992. ∞

Library of Congress Cataloging-in-Publication Data

Neely, Teresa Y.
    Information literacy assessment : standards-based tools and assignments / Teresa Y. Neely ; foreword by Hannelore Rader.
        p.   cm.
    Includes bibliographical references and index.
    ISBN 0-8389-0914-0 (alk. paper)
    1. Information literacy—Standards. 2. Information literacy—Study and teaching (Higher) 3. Information literacy—Ability testing. 4. Library orientation for college students—Evaluation. I. Title.
    ZA3075.N435 2006
    028.7—dc22   2005037186

Printed in the United States of America

10   09   08   5   4   3   2

CONTENTS

FOREWORD

Hannelore Rader

Information literacy has been a topic of much interest both nationally and internationally during the past two decades. In 1989 the American Library Association (ALA) Presidential Committee on Information Literacy published its final report, defining the concept of information literacy and its importance for education, citizens, and the workforce in the information age. The National Forum on Information Literacy was started the same year in Washington, D.C., to provide opportunities for representatives from more than eighty organizations—both profit and nonprofit—to discuss and advance the concept of information literacy nationally. The Institute of Information Literacy was established in 1997 by the Association of College and Research Libraries (ACRL) and is dedicated to playing a leadership role in helping individuals and institutions to integrate information literacy throughout the full spectrum of the educational process. In 1998 the ALA Presidential Committee on Information Literacy issued the *Progress Report on Information Literacy: An Update*. This update clarified the amazing progress that had been made to produce an information-literate population, and it provided six recommendations for further advancement of this important endeavor.

Information literacy has been an important factor in the development of librarian-faculty partnerships to improve students' learning outcomes. Librarians and faculty have worked more closely together in recent times to integrate the teaching of information and technology skills into the entire curriculum. This has been especially significant since the rise of the Internet. As students rely more and more on the electronic environment, they need appropriate information and technology expertise, and librarians together with faculty are providing this important instruction.

Information literacy gained in significance with the ACRL's development in 2000 of the Information Literacy Competency Standards for Higher Education, which gave academic librarians a framework for their instruction. In 2001 the ACRL issued another important set of guidelines, Objectives for Information Literacy Instruction: A Model Statement for Academic Librarians. The ACRL Competency Standards stress that information literacy "forms the basis for lifelong learning," and the "objectives" can be used as a guide for librarians to promote the ACRL Standards at their institutions. A toolkit has also been prepared to provide a step-by-step introduction to each of the five standards, the performance indicators for each standard, and the outcomes for each performance indicator. The standards have been translated into French, Greek, Spanish, and German.

Information literacy has become a global issue during the past decade. National conferences on this topic have been held on every continent, and many publications have been issued as well. It is significant that the International Federation of Library Associations (IFLA) recently created an Information Literacy Section to address information literacy worldwide. Many programs in IFLA's annual conferences have focused on information literacy, and interest in this topic is growing. Educators and librarians in Canada and Australia have been active in information literacy activities similar to those in the United States, holding annual conferences on the topic and publishing articles and books as well. In the United States several organizations are involved with the concept of information literacy, including the American Association of School Libraries, the ACRL Instruction Section, the Library Instruction Roundtable, the National Forum on Information Literacy, and the Teaching, Learning and Technology Affiliate of the American Association of Higher Education. The Library Orientation Exchange, located at Eastern Michigan University, is the national clearinghouse for information literacy materials and since 1972 has sponsored two annual conferences on this topic. Many state library associations also have committees or groups working on information literacy.

Assessing the outcomes of information literacy has been a concern for librarians since the beginning. Recently, however, this concern has gained in strength due to the fact that national accreditation agencies have begun to demand evidence of students' achievements in learning information literacy skills. This book provides a much-needed resource for assessing the learning outcomes of teaching information skills to students in higher education. It is significant that the authors have identified more than seventy survey instruments to help with the assessment of information skills. There is also work in progress to develop national testing instruments for assessing learning outcomes related to information literacy, one example of which is the Educational Testing Service's work on a unique performance-based student assessment instrument for information and communication technology.

There is a real need within the education community to obtain information regarding the assessment of information skills instruction and related learning outcomes. This book provides a good understanding and basis for information literacy testing based on the ACRL Standards. It provides appropriate background information on information literacy, supplies many valuable references to additional information on assessing the information skills of students, and also provides examples of questions from existing testing instruments. This book is indeed a much-needed publication for the library and education community and a major printed guide to assist librarians and faculty in assessing students' information and technology skills.

The Importance of Standards and Assessment

Teresa Y. Neely

T he library profession has long recognized the importance of standards in all aspects of library work. Since 1959 the Association of College and Research Libraries has taken the lead in developing standards and guidelines for academic libraries.[1] The ACRL website notes that the "ACRL is the source that the higher education community looks to for standards and guidelines on academic libraries."[2] The development and widespread acceptance and use of standards is critical in the assessment of student outcomes, especially for information literacy. Librarians in Maryland concluded that in order for students at all levels to succeed academically, they

> must be able to access, retrieve, evaluate, manage, and use information effectively and efficiently from a variety of print and non-print sources. Information resources are multiplying exponentially, and becoming more diverse, more complex, and more interdisciplinary. Successful students must be information literate, as well as technologically proficient, in order to complete basic coursework and degree requirements.[3]

Nowhere else are standards more critical than during the accreditation process. Accreditation is defined as the means of self-regulation and peer review adopted by the educational community.[4] Barbara A. Beno reports that in recent years, accreditation standards developed and used by most of the regional accreditors have changed to incorporate the assessment of student learning as a central process in evaluating institutional effectiveness. The incorporation of student learning outcomes into accreditation evaluation processes reflects a decade-long movement in higher education to assess student learning.[5]

It follows that once standards for student learning have been established, the focus logically turns to assessment. Ilene Rockman notes that "assessment is a process for quality improvement. As such, since libraries are both administrative and academic units, they have an important role to play in the continuous quality improvement goals of their parent organizations."[6] Assessment for libraries is not a new invention, but for some it may require reenvisioning the library's role in assessing student outcomes at the institutional level. Libraries involved with student assessment will have to rethink who, what, how, and in many cases where they are assessing in order to satisfy institutional or external requirements.

Kenneth Smith reminds us that in the shift from the faculty expert model to one that is based on student-realized outcomes, these outcomes include "not only what students know, but also the skills they develop, what they are able to do, and the attitudes of mind that characterize the way they will approach their work over a lifetime of change."[7] Ensuring that students are information literate and prepared for lifelong learning is and has long been a key priority for the profession of librarianship.

Academic accrediting associations and national discipline-specific organizations have begun to lend their weight to the implementation of the ACRL Information Literacy Competency Standards for Higher Education by including information literacy in accreditation guidelines. The Middle States Association of Colleges and Schools has taken a leadership role in this regard, stating that "Information Literacy is vital to all disciplines and to effective teaching and learning in any institution. Institutions of higher education need to provide students and instructors with the knowledge, skills and tools to obtain information in many formats and media."[8]

Although the ACRL did not approve and disseminate the current version of the standards until 2000, a large number of academic institutions and individual researchers had already begun to develop standards for assessing information literacy skills.[9] This trend has continued, and the resulting efforts and findings comprise a body of research that is fractured, with no clear trends or generalizable findings for comparative purposes across academic institutions.

Currently, there are at least two known large-scale efforts under way to develop and implement objective, standardized survey instruments that will produce results that are comparable across campuses, but their initial findings have not yet been publicly disseminated.[10] Additionally, although a significant amount of information literacy assessment is taking place in library and information science education (for dissertations and theses) and in practice, very few of the survey instruments are based on any one set of standards.[11] This book provides a place to begin an assessment-based dialogue about the importance of using a uniform protocol for assessing the baseline information literacy skills of college and university students. It uses the ACRL Standards as a basic framework for developing and implementing an information literacy research agenda at the individual or institutional level, with an eye toward building a body of research literature produced by practitioners and researchers that yields usable, comparable data.

This book fills a gap in the literature on information literacy assessment by providing a link between the standards themselves and the desire to acquire and analyze data from information literacy assessment as a component of institutional assessment for accreditation and self-study purposes.

The authors anticipate the use of this book as a guide to building a culture of information literacy assessment from the grassroots level up through library and university administration.

This book includes a total of ten chapters. Chapter 2 introduces the ACRL Standards and provides a brief discussion of them overall. The chapter includes examples of how to integrate the standards into instruction programs, bibliographic instruction sessions, librarian-taught labs, and stand-alone courses; and there is also a section with tips on developing library-related assignments. Each of chapters 3 through 7 introduces an individual standard, along with its performance indicators and outcomes. Sample assessment queries from institutions in the United States, Canada, and Australia are provided in each chapter, and assignments that represent best practices are also included for many of the performance indicators. These assignments are examples of ways to explain, introduce, and reinforce information literacy concepts and outcomes to students.

Chapter 8 discusses empirically proven areas that have an impact on information literacy assessment but are not explicitly covered by the standards: the nature of the relationship between students and faculty, students' perceptions of and attitudes about the standards, detailed demographic and background information, and technological competencies. This chapter also includes examples of queries designed to assess in some of these areas. Chapter 9 discusses how to develop assessment instruments based on the standards, from garnering institutional support and developing research goals and objectives to writing different types of individual queries. And finally, chapter 10 provides a discussion on the how-to's of automating assessment instruments. This chapter was written specifically for those individuals who may not have the technological skill set to perform certain aspects of instrument automation such as programming or developing a relational database. It is accompanied by a glossary of technical terminology.

During the writing of this book, the authors identified more than seventy survey instruments, which are listed in the appendix. Every effort was made to identify an individual or institution responsible for the survey instruments listed, in order to provide an avenue for requesting copies once the URLs in the appendix are no longer valid. It is the authors' hope that these instruments will provide a starting point for exploring assessment in your own library.

NOTES

1. William N. Nelson and Robert W. Fernekes, "Who Uses ACRL Standards?" *College and Research Libraries News* 66, no. 5 (May 2005): 359.

2. Association of College and Research Libraries, "Standards and Guidelines," http://www.ala.org/ala/acrl/acrlstandards/standardsguidelines.htm.

3. Universities of Maryland Collaborative, "Universities of Maryland Collaborative Information Literacy Grant Proposal" (working paper, 2004).

4. Middle States Commission on Higher Education, *Characteristics of Excellence in Higher Education* (Philadelphia: Middle States Commission on Higher Education, 2002), iv, http://www.msache.org.

5. Barbara A. Beno, "The Role of Student Learning Outcomes in Accreditation Quality Review," *New Directions for Community Colleges*, no. 126 (Summer 2004): 65.

6. Ilene F. Rockman, "The Importance of Assessment," *Reference Services Review* 30, no. 3 (2002): 18.

7. Kenneth R. Smith, "New Roles and Responsibilities for the University Library: Advancing Student Learning through Outcomes Assessment," *ARL*, no. 213 (December 2000): 2.

8. Middle States Commission on Higher Education, *Developing Research and Communication Skills: Guidelines for Information Literacy in the Curriculum* (Philadelphia: Middle States Commission on Higher Education, 2003), 32.

9. See UCLA Instructional Services Advisory Committee, "Instructional Competencies Survey Project, 1997–1998," http://www.bol.ucla.edu/%7Ejherschm/project/presentation .htm; Kathleen Dunn, "Information Competency Assessment: Web-Based Assessment of

University Entry-Level Information Competency" (June 1999), http://www.csupomona .edu/~library/InfoComp/.

10. Lisa G. O'Connor, Carolyn J. Radcliff, and Julie A. Gedeon, "Applying Systems Design and Item Response Theory to the Problem of Measuring Information Literacy Skills," *College and Research Libraries* 63, no. 6 (November 2002): 528–43; Educational Testing Service, "ETS Launches ICT Literacy Assessment, an Online Measure of Student Information and Communication Technology Proficiency," http://www.ets.org/ictliteracy/ educator.html; and Ilene Rockman and Gordon Smith, "National Higher Education Information and Communication Technology (ICT) Initiative: A Unique Partnership," www .calstate.edu/LS/CARL.ppt.

11. See Lut Rahim Nero, "An Assessment of Information Literacy among Graduating Teacher Education Majors of Four Pennsylvania State System of Higher Education (SSHE) Universities" (Ph.D. diss., University of Pittsburgh, 1999); Teresa Yvonne Neely, "Aspects of Information Literacy: A Sociological and Psychological Study" (Ph.D. diss., University of Pittsburgh, 2000); Patricia Davitt Maughan, "Assessing Information Literacy among Undergraduates: A Discussion of the Literature and the University of California-Berkeley Assessment Experience," *College and Research Libraries* 62, no. 1 (January 2001): 71–85; Carol A. Powell and Jane Case-Smith, "Information Literacy Skills of Occupational Therapy Graduates: A Survey of Learning Outcomes," *Journal of the Medical Library Association* 91, no. 4 (October 2003): 468–78; and Molly R. Flaspohler, "Information Literacy Program Assessment: One Small College Takes the Big Plunge," *Reference Services Review* 31, no. 2 (2003): 129–40. Flaspohler's study used the ACRL Standards to develop interventions, but the survey instrument was developed at the UCLA Libraries based on standards developed in 1998; see http://www.bol.ucla.edu/~jherschm/project/.

Integrating the ACRL Standards

Teresa Y. Neely and Katy Sullivan

In this chapter, we will provide an overview of the Information Literacy Competency Standards for Higher Education developed by the Association of College and Research Libraries. We will discuss how the standards can be integrated into information literacy, user education, and instruction programs overall, as well as into bibliographic instruction sessions, librarian-taught labs, and stand-alone courses.

This chapter will also provide an introduction and overview of the next five chapters, each of which outlines and provides an in-depth discussion of one standard, along with its accompanying performance indicators and outcomes.

THE STANDARDS

In January 2000 the ACRL approved the final version of the standards, which were developed by the ACRL Task Force on Information Literacy Competency Standards. The goal of the task force was to provide a framework to assist and guide the development of information-literate individuals. The final product included 5 standards, 22 performance indicators, and more than 100 outcomes intended to provide some insight into the skill set needed during the research process.

The five ACRL Standards are as follows:

1. The information literate student determines the nature and extent of information needed.
2. The information literate student accesses needed information effectively and efficiently.
3. The information literate student evaluates information and its sources critically and incorporates selected information into his or her knowledge base and value system.
4. The information literate student, individually or as a member of a group, uses information effectively to accomplish a specific purpose.
5. The information literate student understands the economic, legal, and social issues surrounding the use of information and accesses and uses information ethically and legally.[1]

Each of chapters 3 through 7 in this book will address one of the five standards. The chapter structure will follow that used by the ACRL, in that each standard will be replicated with its accompanying performance indicators, followed by outcomes. The sequence uses a series of numbers and letters to identify individual indicators and outcomes. For example, the first performance indicator for Standard 1 is numbered 1.1, and the first few outcomes for this indicator are labeled 1.1.a, 1.1.b., 1.1.c, and so on.

The standards and many of their accompanying performance indicators and outcomes are broadly written and, because of this, can be measured using alternative methods of assessment that may be more sophisticated and complex than the survey method approach discussed in this book. Active course-learning techniques, audiovisual aids, collaborative learning exercises, debates, focused library activities, and so on are other methods of assessment that can be used to determine student outcomes in the context of information literacy.

Queries and Assignments

Each chapter on a standard will include a discussion of writing, developing, and adapting queries for each standard. These queries are designed to assess students' proficiency at the performance indicators for each standard. The Information Literacy Task Force at the University of Maryland, Baltimore County (UMBC), identified and reviewed more than seventy information literacy survey instruments. (See the appendix.) Some queries that represent best practices for the standards were taken from or adapted from these surveys. Examples from these surveys are also represented in chapter 9 in the discussion of types of queries.

Each chapter on a standard also includes examples of assignments designed to assist students in the acquisition, development, and reinforcement of the skills represented by that standard. The UMBC Task Force made every effort to identify the creators of the assignments, but in some cases the author could not be determined.

Categorization

Inevitably a discussion of the instruction, acquisition, and mastery of information literacy skills will turn to a discussion of taxonomies, rubrics, and a systematic categorization of individual skills based on knowledge and development. It is our belief, however, that assigning the standards, performance indicators, and outcomes a fixed spot in a taxonomy table would be highly subjective, based on the task force's perceptions of which skills should be placed where. Therefore, in this book, we do not categorize the skills into a taxonomy intended to differentiate between higher-order and lower-order skills.

Many of the skills set forth in the standards can be addressed and acquired at a variety of levels, depending on the level of research being conducted and the expected outcome of the research (e.g., research paper, presentation). Each chapter in this book will identify and address the distinction between higher- and lower-order skills accordingly, where relevant. We believe that the skills set forth in the standards are merely a starting point for all individuals, which in the case of a college campus includes faculty, staff, and college-level students. The skills can and should be assessed and included in instruction at the various levels. For example, chapter 4 addresses a performance indicator and outcomes according to which information-literate students "extract, record, and manage information and its sources." Undergraduate students can accomplish this task by using the cut-and-paste function in word-processing and Windows software, or by e-mailing, saving, or downloading citations to relevant resources. Upper-level undergraduates and graduate students, however, depending upon the assignment or course requirement, may find it necessary to master personal bibliographic management software in order to organize and manage the information resources they have gathered. Thus, the nature of the standards and the varying levels of college-level students' information literacy exposure severely limits the ability to uniformly categorize the standards for assessment purposes.

INTEGRATING THE STANDARDS

Most of the ACRL Standards can be integrated into formal library instruction relatively easily, allowing you to cover most of your bases and be assured of including the key issues in the library research process. In most cases, it will not be necessary to integrate all of the standards at one time. Instead, determine which of the standards and outcomes are appropriate for your purposes and begin at that point.

The integration of the standards, like the integration of most library research skills, is most effective when done in the context of student learning. Most student learning occurs in the classroom; however, there are instances of student learning where librarians are involved.

Course-Integrated Instruction

This type of bibliographic instruction is the most common in academic libraries. Typically, the faculty member arranges to bring the class to the library to receive instruction in one or more areas, such as locating scholarly journal articles, finding biographical information, or evaluating web pages. In other cases, the librarian may visit the classroom to provide instruction. Regardless of whether the students visit the library or the librarian visits the classroom, integration of the standards depends primarily on the intended outcomes for that session—that is, what the faculty member expects the librarian to teach the students.

For example, let us assume that students are supposed to research a topic relating to the health of African-Americans. The faculty member acknowledges that students previously had relied heavily on Internet resources to complete this assignment. She wants them to be introduced to reputable Internet sites, as well as the scholarly journal literature.

In developing the library session for this course, standard integration, based on the assignment and the course needs, can be accomplished as outlined below. First we describe the stage in the research project, citing the outcome that will be integrated, and then we identify the librarian's role, if any, at that stage.

1. Identify a health-related issue for African-Americans. (*Outcome 1.1.a. Confers with instructors and participates in class discussions, peer workgroups, and electronic discussions to identify a research topic, or other information need*)

    Librarian's role: None; student/course-initiated.

2. Develop research questions based on topic. (*Outcome 1.1.b. Develops a thesis statement and formulates questions based on the information need*)

    Librarian's role: None; student/course-initiated.

3. Identify and review general resources to become familiar with topic. (*Outcome 1.1.c. Explores general information sources to increase familiarity with the topic*)

    Librarian's role: Introduce students to the concept of using general information resources such as subject encyclopedias, dictionaries, and handbooks to become familiar with their topic.

4. Identify key words and concepts to describe topic. (*Outcome 1.1.e. Identifies key concepts and terms that describe the information need*)

    Librarian's role: Brainstorm with students to identify key concepts that help to describe topic: for example, high blood pressure versus hypertension; AIDS versus acquired immune deficiency syndrome; sugar versus diabetes.

5. Identify a variety of types, formats, and sources of information. (*Outcome 1.2.a. Knows how information is formally and informally produced, organized, and disseminated*)

    Librarian's role: A brief lecture on how information is produced, organized, and disseminated; how the major academic disciplines influence the production, organization and dissemination of information; the variety of types and formats of information (e.g., multimedia, database, website, data set, audiovisual, book); the variety of sources of information; the purpose and audience of potential resources (e.g., popular vs. scholarly, current vs. historical). Brainstorm with students about the types and formats of resources that would be most appropriate for their particular health issue (e.g., journal articles, websites).

6. (*Outcomes 2.1.a–d. Selects the most appropriate investigative methods or information retrieval systems for accessing the needed information*)

Librarian's role (may be limited by faculty members' expectations and course goals and objectives): A brief lecture on identifying and selecting an appropriate database for health-related issues. Introduce and do sample searching in the library's catalog; general databases such as *Academic Search Premier* or *Masterfile Premier*; and subject-specific databases such as *Medline* and *PsycINFO*. Also, include a discussion on Internet resources including professional associations (American Medical Association, Association of Black Psychologists), government (Centers for Disease Control and Prevention, National Institutes of Health), education (Joslin Diabetes Center—affiliated with Harvard Medical School), and commercial websites (WebMD.com). Provide opportunity for hands-on searching. Student's role: in-class assignment: Select the library's catalog or a subject database and/or websites for the particular health issue and focus of the assignment.

7. (*Outcomes 2.2.a–f. Constructs and implements effectively designed search strategies*)

Librarian's role: A brief lecture on developing successful search strategies, including controlled vocabulary and subject headings, Boolean logic, and other search strategies. Student's role: Participate in identifying appropriate keywords/subject headings for their topics using various resources (library catalogs, databases, descriptors, thesauri, subject headings). Practice searching using these terms in the database(s) selected in step 6.

8. (*Outcomes 2.3.a–c. Retrieves information online or in person using a variety of methods*)

Librarian's role: A brief lecture on retrieving located information, including using the local online catalog and/or serials database to determine ownership and journal subscription information and to determine call numbers and locations in the stacks, e.g., Library of Congress call number classification, Superintendent of Documents call numbers, local call number schema, etc.; retrieving full-text and print-based materials; interlibrary loan (ILL), resource-sharing agreements, and document delivery services. Student's role: After identifying journal articles and books, determine whether the library owns the items and describe how to go about obtaining the items.

9. (*Outcome 3.2.a. Articulates and applies initial criteria for evaluating both the information and its sources*)

> Librarian's role: A brief lecture on evaluating information, including websites and information found in databases, e.g., journal articles. Student's role: Apply evaluative criteria to the items they have identified and participate in a discussion of the usefulness and appropriateness of the resources for completing the assignment.

This particular instruction session lasted about two and a half hours; however, most lectures average about fifty minutes, and you will not be able to cover this much ground. Additionally, the instructor may only allow part of the total course time for library instruction. It is important to acknowledge that you may not be able to cover all the topics you want to as comprehensively as you might like. You may need to provide detailed handouts or develop a web page so that students have something to refer to, as well as to provide the information that you are unable to cover. The development of individual web pages for individual courses or sessions can be time-consuming and difficult to manage over time, given the potential number of bibliographic sessions taught in a typical semester. It may be more appropriate to develop a template for subject or research guides that lends itself to instructional purposes. For example, a subject guide for psychology could include databases, print reference resources, appropriate associations and organizations, and links to meta sites with additional information. Depending upon your audience, it may be advantageous to develop subject or research guides for specific diverse groups. In this instance, students completing research on topics relating to the health of African-Americans could be referred to the guides on African-Americans and psychology, and the session could be used to focus on specific skills (standards) of interest.

When integrating the standards into bibliographic instruction sessions, it is important to keep in mind the faculty members' priorities and make sure they are addressed. This will ensure that the students have the information needed to adequately complete their assignment. In addition, you should always provide your e-mail address and phone number so that students may contact you after the session in case they need additional assistance.

Librarian-Developed Courses

A host of these courses are widely available, ranging from one-credit partial-semester to three-credit semester-long courses. Integrating the standards into these courses may require an overhaul and revision of the syllabus, much like the revision of a course offered in a particular academic discipline. This begins with a review and possible revision of the course goals and objectives. It cannot be assumed that the average library research methods course will be in compliance with the standards, so all aspects of the course and syllabus must be reviewed and revised, if necessary.

Librarians at the University of Maryland, Baltimore County, revised two course syllabi to incorporate the standards: one for a three-credit course developed and taught by librarians for the Honors College—Honors 201 and one for an eight-week librarian-taught lab offered in conjunction with a three-credit course for the Ronald E. McNair Scholars program—Research Proposal Fundamentals (AFST 495). The following is a description of the syllabus revision process for the eight-week lab course.

AFST 495

Prior to integrating the standards into this eight-week lab, it was determined that the management of the course needed to be addressed. At that time, each reference librarian in the department was teaching a different session. To streamline the process and make more productive use of the librarians' time, two librarians volunteered to teach the course. The course syllabus previously had been organized around resources and functions as is shown below. After integration, the course syllabus flowed from and built upon the standards and their performance indicators.

AFST 495 prior to Standards Integration

> Week 1. Introduction to staff, course objectives, library services; the nature of research
>
> Week 2. Evaluating material identified; organizing information
>
> Week 3. Online catalogs/electronic sources
>
> Week 4. Printed/online reference sources
>
> Week 5. Online/printed indexes and abstracts
>
> Week 6. Statistics and government documents
>
> Week 7. World Wide Web and critical thinking
>
> Week 8. Capstone session

AFST 495 after Standards Integration

Week 1. Introduction, course overview, and discussion of information literacy as a concept (viewed *E-literate?* video), discussion of research topics[2]

Week 2. Performance Indicator 1.1, Indicator 1.2
- How knowledge is organized
- Types of resources and formats available
- Defining and articulating research needs

Week 3. Indicator 2.1, Indicator 2.2, Indicator 2.4, Indicator 2.5, Indicator 3.2
- Select the most appropriate resources
  Catalogusmai (local catalog) and *WorldCat*
  Subject databases for journal articles
  Serial search (local serials database)
- Access information efficiently and effectively
- Retrieve information in a variety of ways
- Criteria for evaluation
- Refine search strategy

Week 4. Indicator 2.1, Indicator 2.2, Indicator 2.3, Indicator 2.5, Indicator 3.2
- Controlled vocabulary
- Implementing and refining search strategy
  Using keywords and descriptors
  Boolean searching
  Proximity/phrase searching
- Evaluating materials you find
  Author
  Publisher/publication
  Bias
  Currency
  References to other sources
  Reliability
- E-mailing/saving/printing

Week 5. Indicator 3.1, Indicator 3.2, Indicator 3.3, Indicator 3.4, Indicator 3.7, Indicator 5.1
- Evaluating and incorporating information
- Rewriting of original thesis
- Academic integrity and plagiarism
- Citation style guides

Week 6. Indicator 4.1, Indicator 4.2, Indicator 4.3
- Presentation techniques
- Information use and issues in using information

Week 7. Indicator 5.1, Indicator 5.2, Indicator 5.3
- Information use and issues in using information
- Course presentations

Week 8. Indicator 5.2, Indicator 5.3
- Information use and issues in using information
- Course presentations
- Course wrap-up/course evaluations

For this course, the instructors felt it was important to introduce the concept of information literacy to the students and to facilitate a discussion on the students' perceptions of and knowledge about information literacy. The instructors used a video to introduce the concept and jump-start the discussion.[3] The syllabus was revised to map the standards to areas that could be covered in eight fifty-minute sessions.

Some of these sessions had to be adjusted due to mitigating factors such as taking attendance, distributing and collecting assignments, hands-on time, and class discussions. The instructors found that in some cases they were unable to spend a great deal of time on all of the topics; however, a brief lecture along with some structured hands-on exercises proved to be just as effective as a twenty-minute lecture on an individual topic. The instructors found that flexibility was key in the management of the course. For example, if after a lecture and discussion, students were unable to adequately complete an assignment, it was necessary to revisit that topic. This sometimes meant that topics were occasionally bumped to the next session.

When integrating the standards into your instruction sessions, remember to focus on the standard, not the resources. You will find that you are still teaching the same concepts, but your focus has shifted to ensuring that students understand how to identify a database for their appropriate topic, rather than you picking one and demonstrating it. If you focus on the standards, the resources will logically follow, as is seen in the revision of AFST 495 above. Students will understand the process of identifying a topic, learning more about the topic, and identifying the most appropriate investigative method, information retrieval system (e.g., selecting a database), and so on. Once the students have been introduced to and understand this process, and their skills have been reinforced, they can transfer those skills to other courses, libraries, and information-literate environments in the pursuit of graduate and other degrees and into the workforce.

Assignment Development

Some assignments are appropriate for more than one area of the standards. In the process of identifying assignments, the task force found that most websites and published literature focused on and offered tips for creating good assignments as opposed to actual library assignments. The tips, usually aimed at faculty, consist of the advice librarians have been attempting to share with faculty for decades.

Evidence shows that when instructors clearly state assignment requirements in writing, the chances of students completing the assignments successfully increase greatly. When an economics professor grew tired of receiving assignments with more and more web-based resources—many of them commercial—he mandated in the syllabus that students use at least five peer-reviewed sources in their research.[4] But he is in the minority. In her 2001 article on library assignments, Necia Parker-Gibson notes the situation and design problems related to library assignments that pose problems for students. "Too frequently library assignments are empty exercises for which neither the student nor the teacher has much sense of purpose. Assignments must be designed to create a need for information that is felt on a personal level."[5]

In developing successful creative assignments, it is a good idea to remember what motivates students:

- a need to know (curiosity about the subject matter)
- relevance of the assignment to the course content and other assignments
- perceived value in knowing the material

- lively modeling of the process by the professor or librarian
- an expected level of success with the assignment[6]

Some other areas to consider are the following.

Provide assignment objectives. Inform students of the learning objectives of the assignment. Tell students why they are doing the assignment and the purpose it serves. An effective assignment relates to some aspect of the subject of the class and increases understanding of the material through the process of researching and locating related information.

Clarify the assignment requirements and expectations. State the requirements in writing as well as verbally. Assignment requirements should be written clearly and simply; and time should be allotted to allow students the opportunity to ask questions and to clarify any information that is ambiguous or unclear.

Describe the specifics of the assignment. Do you want the students to cite in a specific style, such as APA (American Psychological Association) or MLA (Modern Language Association)? Are there specific types of resources that are acceptable while others are not? Make sure to convey this to students in writing and provide examples if possible.

Distinguish between resources. When describing the requirements of an assignment, distinguish between different types of sources: popular and scholarly, primary and secondary, and so on. If possible, show examples.

Check for feasibility. Make sure the library's resources are adequate for the assignment. If you expect the students to use resources from other libraries, make sure they are aware of it and know how to access these resources.

Check the assignment beforehand. Ideally, it is best to test the assignment yourself. Try to approach it from your students' perspectives and experiences. If you have created an extremely challenging assignment that is difficult for you to complete, your students will not be successful, and the experience could prove to be frustrating and destructive.

Do not assume students already know the basics. Many college students have little (if any) experience completing assignments and course work using a college or university library. There is significant empirical evidence that reveals that the majority of people first learn to use the library in grade school or high school.[7] Assume minimal knowledge of library resources, procedures, and jargon.

Allow variety in topic selection. Allowing your students to research a variety of topics prevents a "mob scene" in the library. If the whole class must depend on one or a few sources, those sources may be mutilated or eventually disappear.

Foster critical thinking. Encourage a critical approach to doing research. Develop assignments that require students to integrate knowledge from a variety of sources rather than relying on just one source and encourage them to evaluate everything they find.

Allow for incremental improvement. Allow students to begin working on the project early in the semester and to work on small assignments (such as turning in an initial bibliography of resources) throughout the semester. Give feedback.

Keep your assignments current. Library resources are constantly in flux—check your assignments each semester so that your students are not asked to use outdated resources or methods of research.

Get to know your reference and instruction librarians—Many academic libraries assign librarians as liaisons to academic departments. Librarians can assist you in identifying resources, developing assignments, and introducing students to library resources and services.

NOTES

1. ACRL Task Force on Information Literacy Competency Standards, "Information Literacy Competency Standards for Higher Education: The Final Version, Approved January 2000," *College and Research Libraries News* 61, no. 3 (March 2000): 207–15.

2. *E-literate?* videocassette, produced by Thomas Eberhardt, 9 min. (Pacific Bell/ University of California, Los Angeles, Graduate School of Education and Information Studies, 2000).

3. *E-literate?*

4. Philip M. Davis, "Effect of the Web on Undergraduate Citation Behavior: Guiding Student Scholarship in a Networked Age," *Portal: Libraries and the Academy* 3, no. 1 (2003): 41–51.

5. Necia Parker-Gibson, "Library Assignments: Challenges That Students Face and How to Help," *College Teaching* 49, no. 2 (2001): 65.

6. Parker-Gibson, "Library Assignments." See also M. D. Svinicki and B. A. Schwartz, *Designing Instruction for Library Users: A Practical Guide* (New York: M. Dekker, 1988).

7. Teresa Yvonne Neely, "Aspects of Information Literacy: A Sociological and Psychological Study" (Ph.D. diss., University of Pittsburgh, 2000), 150–51.

Developing a Topic and Identifying Sources of Information

Katy Sullivan

STANDARD 1
The information literate student determines the nature and
extent of the information needed.

Standard 1 addresses two major areas of information literacy: the ability to recognize and define an information need and the ability to identify a variety of types and formats of potential sources of information. These abilities are crucial in the early stages of the research process, of which many aspects are overlooked by college-level students. These early stages are essential for successful research, and students should be encouraged to develop their skills in these areas. This can be done by using carefully developed assignments that are given in tandem with a research topic and major assignment, such as a research paper. The assignment examples in this chapter are presented as guides and may be adapted to fit your institution's particular needs. Well-planned information literacy instruction will assist students in developing the skills needed for successful lifelong learning.

Although this standard has four performance indicators and seventeen accompanying outcomes, the primary concepts for college students are the ability to recognize and define an information need (1.1) and the ability to understand and identify a variety of types and formats of potential information sources (1.2). This standard includes both higher-order skills, such as constructing information with raw data from primary sources (1.1.f), and lower-order skills, such as developing a thesis statement and formulating questions based on information needs (1.1.b).

ASSESSING THE ABILITY TO DEFINE INFORMATIONAL NEEDS

Performance Indicator 1.1. The information literate student defines and articulates the need for information.

> *Outcome 1.1.a*. Confers with instructors and participates in class discussions, peer workgroups, and electronic discussions to identify a research topic, or other information need

> *Outcome 1.1.b*. Develops a thesis statement and formulates questions based on the information need

> *Outcome 1.1.c*. Explores general information sources to increase familiarity with the topic

> *Outcome 1.1.d*. Defines or modifies the information need to achieve a manageable focus

> *Outcome 1.1.e*. Identifies key concepts and terms that describe the information need

> *Outcome 1.1.f*. Recognizes that existing information can be combined with original thought, experimentation, and/or analysis to produce new information

For college-level students, the step of defining and articulating the need for information is often underaddressed or overlooked entirely. Frequently, the determination of an information need is not the decision of the student. More often, college-level students must investigate an information need in order to satisfy a course requirement. The instructor gives an assignment such as a research paper, and the student conducts library research in order to complete that assignment. In most college courses the assignment is tied to the subject matter of the course. Topic selection and accompanying research questions are often decided for the student as well. Upper-level undergraduates and graduate students are generally allowed more freedom in topic selection and more initiative in defining and articulating an information need. However, most undergraduates do not enjoy this opportunity. This is an issue because too often students themselves are not required to see problems or identify information needs. This impedes the development of problem-solving and critical thinking skills. For many students, it is difficult to accept that the early stages of the research process are not always direct and straightforward, and this may cause feelings of anxiety and unease. It is much more advantageous for students to approach this part of the process as a discovery stage, sometimes circuitous, seldom direct. Faculty and librarians can assist students at this stage by discussing topic ideas, talking about reference sources, and providing assignments that encourage students to examine their ideas and potential sources of information.

Assessment Queries

One way to broadly assess the first indicator for Standard 1 is to introduce students to hypothetical situations and inquire whether or not those situations require the use of information.

> We need information when we want to
>> a. discuss current issues
>> b. plan a vacation
>> c. write a report
>> d. revise our diet
>> e. answers a, b, c, and d[1]

Too often the library research and discovery process is introduced and reinforced to the student in isolation from everyday life. This type of question illustrates that the need for information is evident in all aspects of life, not just when the student is faced with a research assignment.

Another query that broadly assesses 1.1 was developed by Claudia J. Morner for her doctoral research. Morner's dissertation produced the *Morner Test of Library Research Skills* (*Morner Test*).

> What is the most important first step in library research?
>> a. identify key authors on research problem
>> b. know research problem
>> c. locate key articles on research problem
>> d. locate key books on research problem

In order to be successful with the research process, students must first understand their research needs. The question above addresses the tendency of many students to focus on collecting sources of information before they really understand their information needs or have refined their research topics. It would be useful to add a fifth possible answer, "I don't know," to prevent students from simply guessing.

In terms of formulating a research question, and identifying keywords, the Cabrillo College *Information Literacy Assessment* uses a more qualitative approach. Students are first asked to write a research question from a broad topic. A second query asks students to identify keywords based on the research question. The electronic version of this assessment query includes a text box for answer submission. Depending on the number of students you are assessing, this short-answer format may not be the best approach, but it is an excellent way to find out exactly how students are approaching their topics and what keywords they are using.

> *Forming a research question from a broad topic.* Let's say that you wanted to research the topic "computer and Internet crimes." Given that broad area of interest, what might be a research question to investigate—for example, "Should governments get involved in regulating the use of the Internet?"
>
> *Identifying keywords.* Using the research question you drafted above, what keywords might be good to use in the first stages of research? (If you didn't write your own research question, use the question given in the example.)

With the exception of a vague reference in performance indicator 3.6, Standard 1 is the only one that addresses students' relationships with faculty and instructors (1.1.a). The following query, taken from the *Albin O. Kuhn Library & Gallery Information Literacy Survey (UMBC Survey)*, investigates a student's comfort level in asking his or her professor for assistance. This is an attitudinal question that addresses an issue that students may not be comfortable with. Many faculty members are unaware that some students may find approaching them for assistance to be intimidating or difficult. (For additional discussion on student-faculty relationships, see chapter 8.)

> To what extent do you feel comfortable asking your professors for assistance in locating resources to support your research? Please select all that apply.

a. I feel comfortable setting up an appointment with a professor for in-depth consultation regarding resources.

b. I feel comfortable asking my professors for a few recommended titles/authors in the field.

c. I don't feel comfortable asking professors for assistance in this area.

d. I have never needed a professor's assistance in locating resources.

Successful researchers develop research questions based on their need for information (1.1.b), and they know how to refine a broad topic into a narrow, manageable one (1.1.d). One way to assess whether students understand how to do this is to provide them with a series of related questions and ask which one is appropriate for a broad topic.

You need to research an aspect of the topic "education in public schools." Which one of the following would be an appropriate research question?

a. Does bilingual education help children attending public schools?

b. Should all schoolchildren receive free lunches?

c. Should states require standardized testing for religious schools?

d. Do labor unions help teachers keep their jobs?[2]

Students who understand how research questions develop from an information need would select response a. The other options are off topic, focusing on lunch programs rather than education and learning, religious schools rather than public schools, and teachers' unions rather than education itself. Again, an option for "I don't know" might prevent students from guessing.

Standard 1 also addresses the use of reference sources during the research process (1.1.c). If used, reference sources prove to be excellent tools for providing an overview of a topic and explanations of key concepts. Often these sources provide terminology that can be used to search databases and catalogs. An article from a subject encyclopedia, succinct and written in nontechnical terms, can be very helpful for students who are researching something new or unfamiliar. Frequently, students do not have even a basic grasp of their research topics. A simple piece of background literature can also help relieve the stress of a student overwhelmed by a large number of potential resources and an unfamiliar topic. All too often students get bogged down in details and are not comfortable with the somewhat ambiguous nature of a process in which flexibility and the ability to alter one's topic and source needs are helpful. The question below was taken from the Florida Gulf Coast University Library's *Search for the Skunk Ape (Information Literacy Tutorial)*, or *FGC Skunk Ape Tutorial*, and addresses outcome 1.1.c.

> You have gotten an assignment on a topic about which you know very little. What's the first thing you should do to get started?
>
> a. Browse the library shelves for books on your topic.
>
> b. Ask the professor if you can change topics.
>
> c. Find out some basics on your topic from a reference source such as an encyclopedia.
>
> d. Ask your friends if any of them know about your topic.

The following query also addresses outcome 1.1.c.

> You are writing a paper for your ecology class. You first need information defining the term "watershed." What is your best choice for getting some brief background information?
>
> a. Search for "watershed" in the library's online catalog.
>
> b. Find journal articles about "watershed."
>
> c. Look up "watershed" in a general reference source like an encyclopedia.
>
> d. Type "watershed" in a web search engine for a complete list of references on the topic.[3]

In addition to determining whether students are familiar with reference sources and regularly use them for background information, this question also requires students to possess some knowledge about the type of information that can be found in the library's online catalog, journal articles, and on the Web. Additionally, it assumes that students know what an online catalog is and how different it is from what they may find on the Web or in journal articles. The question also does not mention the words *database* or *article index*, and this omission may confuse some novice library users who are not familiar with where they can "Find journal articles." It might also be useful to specify a subject encyclopedia as an option, rather than a general encyclopedia, considering that subject-oriented reference sources are more appropriate for college-level learning. A fifth option of "I don't know" is also recommended.

The following is an assessment query taken from the *Neely Test of Relevance, Evaluation, and Information Literacy Attitudes* (*Neely Test*) that asks students about the use of sources when researching a particular topic. This question was adapted and expanded from an item appearing in the *Morner Test*. Not only does a query of this type ascertain whether or not students use reference sources, but it can determine whether or not they are using them at the right time during the research process (in the beginning). The options for this question can be changed to other activities, such as "discuss your topic with your professor," to suit the needs of your institution. This query also assesses outcomes 1.1.d and 1.1.e.

> "Violence in American high schools" is a popular topic because it is a growing problem. Given this topic as the subject of a research project, in what order would you perform these steps? (1–the first step; 2–the second step, etc.; use 0 if you would not take a particular step)
>
> a. Browse a current printed magazine index.
> b. Browse the most recent issue of an education journal.
> c. Search the Internet using the keywords "violence" and "high schools."
> d. Look at reference material that provides an overview of "violence and teenagers."
> e. Brainstorm the concept, using the terms in the topic.
> f. Formulate questions based on the information needed to begin the research.
> g. Search subject-based and other related databases.

One element of the first performance indicator is an understanding of the importance of identifying key concepts and terms that describe an information need (1.1.e). These concepts can be used for online searching on the Web and in databases, among other things. The *Neely Test* adapted the following question from the *Morner Test* as well.

> Before searching for information on a topic, such as "adolescent drug use in urban schools," you would first
>
> a. decide which databases or indexes are appropriate for the search
> b. divide the topic into concepts or terms
> c. know which aspects of the topic are most important

  d. revise the topic to be more specific

  e. I don't know

One of the first steps in the research process is to determine the major concepts or terms related to a topic. It is essential for students to perform this step before they begin searching in order to have useful keywords. Once they begin searching, it may be necessary to revise the topic to be more specific if it is determined the topic is too broad (3.7).

Assignments

As stated before, one of the major components of Standard 1 is the process of determining useful keywords. Students consistently struggle with this step, frequently skipping it entirely. Anecdotal evidence gathered from reference librarians reveals that many students do not know how to focus and develop their topics into something that would lend itself to enough, but not too much, research. Carol Kuhlthau found that of the users she studied, "half of the users in academic, public and secondary school libraries studied did not show evidence of reaching a focused perspective of their topic at any time during the search process."[4] Although it may come as a surprise to some, many students complete an entire research paper without ever going through the process of refining their topic and determining major search concepts.

  How can this skill be developed and encouraged? On a very casual level, a student can discuss his or her topic with professors and classmates, which can help to identify other viewpoints and ideas (1.1.a). Exploring reference sources for background information is also helpful (1.1.c). Instructors can assist students in tackling these steps by assigning an exercise that requires them to formulate research questions based on their given topics and to define keywords, concepts, and synonyms related to their topics.

  One such exercise has been used by the California Polytechnic State University System.[5] This assignment is similar in format and focus to the qualitative-type query from Cabrillo College discussed earlier. The assignment includes an online tutorial that takes students through the early stages of the research process. Students are asked to first state their topic as a research question in order to clarify their thoughts. Second, students are asked to identify the main concepts in the questions. For example, a topic such as drinking and driving would lend itself to research questions such as "How does drinking affect driving?" and "What are the laws regulating drinking and driving?" Key concepts taken from these questions are drinking, driving, affect, and laws. Students can then create lists of synonyms and related words for each of the concepts. The concept of drinking has synonyms and related words that include alcoholism, intoxication, inebriation, and substance abuse. Finally, students are asked to look critically at their research questions and determine if they need to broaden or narrow their topic. Students may need to refine their topic by adding concrete or specific terms to their questions. This last step may require them to determine a new list of concepts, synonyms, and related terms. In small classes, instructors can use this as an opportunity to encourage classroom discussion by having students discuss their topics in class (1.1.a), work together to formulate research questions (1.1.b), and determine key concepts (1.1.e). Larger classes can be assigned this exercise as a take-home assignment with follow-up written feedback from the instructor or in-class peer review. This exercise can also be used to address Standard 2 by having students develop search statements using search strategies (2.2), for example, by inserting Boolean operators between the concepts. (See chapter 4 for additional discussion on search strategies.)

Another way to assist students in defining and articulating an information need is to have them develop a concept map. Concept mapping is a technique used for a variety of purposes, including generating new ideas, designing complex structures, communicating complex ideas, and assessing understanding or diagnosing misunderstanding. For undergraduates working on the initial stages of research, this technique can greatly assist students in analyzing and focusing their topics, thereby avoiding the need to spend excess time in the subsequent stages of research (specifically in database and web searching). If students are unfamiliar with their topics, it may be useful to have them do background reading on their topics using appropriate reference sources before completing this activity.

When developing a concept map, the first step is to determine the central word, concept, or research question around which to build the map. From there, students can add associated concepts, items, descriptive words, and even questions. A concept map can be developed using a top-down approach, working from general to specific, or with more of a brainstorming approach, using free association. Students can use different colors and shapes to identify different types of information. Figure 3-1 is an example of a concept map developed by the author for the topic of vegetarianism.

There are many benefits to doing such an exercise. It requires a student to think about his or her topic and any issues that surround that topic. The

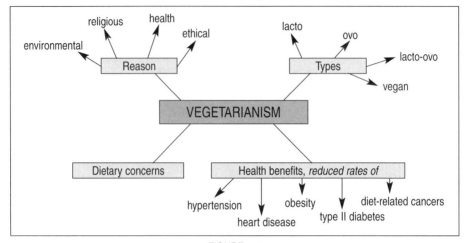

FIGURE 3-1
Concept Map for "Vegetarianism"

more that students analyze their topics, the more focused they can be while doing their research. Developing a concept map is a great way for students to determine key concepts and terms that describe their information needs. The sample map starts with a very broad topic and focuses the topic using major headings and subheadings. When completing this assignment, students should be encouraged to begin by writing down all of the words that they associate with their broader concepts, no matter how unrelated those concepts may seem. They do not need to limit themselves at this point in their research. This is an exercise in exploration, but it should not take the place of a traditional, linear outline.

ASSESSING THE ABILITY TO IDENTIFY TYPES OF INFORMATION SOURCES

Performance Indicator 1.2. The information literate student identifies a variety of types and formats of potential sources for information.

> ***Outcome 1.2.a.*** Knows how information is formally and informally produced, organized, and disseminated
>
> ***Outcome 1.2.b.*** Recognizes that knowledge can be organized into disciplines that influence the way information is accessed

In order to master performance indicator 1.2, it is essential for students to understand how information is "produced, organized, and disseminated." This involves understanding that information can be divided into broad categories by discipline (science, social science, humanities) and that this affects the way information is accessed. It is essential for students to realize that different disciplines produce and organize their literature in different ways. For example, the usefulness of information in the sciences is generally dependent on that information's currency. The most cutting-edge research is frequently available in the form of conference proceedings or online sources, rather than in books or journal articles. In the humanities, subject areas such as history and literature are dependent on older materials as well as new, and books are frequently cited in scholarly research. Morner's dissertation research revealed that even doctoral-level students do not always understand the publication cycle and how it relates to various formats, and this adds to their confusion in the library.[6]

Assessment Queries

The *Morner Test* produced the following two assessment queries for outcomes 1.2.a and b.

The first place most research in education appears is

  a. in books published by university presses

  b. in education encyclopedia articles

  c. in newsletters of professional organizations

  d. at professional conferences and journal articles

Although this question was developed for education students, it could be adapted for any subject or discipline.

The best way to get a copy of a paper given at a December 1992 education conference is to

  a. search *ERIC* under the author's name

  b. wait until it appears in a journal

  c. write to the author for a copy

  d. write to professional associations that sponsored the conference

In addition to addressing outcomes 1.2.a and b, this question includes an option about a leading article database in the education field and introduces the concept of the possibility of interaction between the presenter/author and the information seeker (2.3.c, 3.6), a concept that college-level students may not have considered as part of the information-seeking process.

Assignments

Many students do not have a thorough understanding of the scholarly publishing cycle. Without this understanding, it is difficult for students to comprehend that there may be a great deal of time between an author's initial research inquiries and final publication of the results of the research. This assignment requires students to investigate the publishing cycle. Students must identify an experimental article from a journal and then attempt to answer the following:

- The earliest date of the author's interest in this research
- The first date the author gathered experimental data for the paper
- Whether or not a scholarship or grant was awarded for the research
- If an earlier version of the paper was presented or published, and when
- When the paper was first received at the journal
- When the revisions were received at the journal
- When the final version was received at the journal
- When the final version was published
- How much time elapsed between the time data were gathered and the final version was published, and if this is significant

This assignment illustrates that the scholarly publication cycle may be quite long and that different types of information are produced and available at different stages of the cycle. Students must consider what happens before publication and when something becomes part of recorded knowledge. Students may also need to use some fairly unorthodox techniques (for them), such as contacting an author, editor, or publisher in order to answer all of the questions adequately. A weakness of this assignment is that all questions may not be answerable, depending upon the publication and the availability of the author(s).

Frequently students have only a limited knowledge of the literature of a particular discipline—they are unfamiliar with the major authors and journals of the field and do not understand the structure of scholarly research.[7] One way to assist students in understanding this process is to have them investigate the production and dissemination of information in a given discipline. In determining what the literature of a particular discipline or subject "looks like," students should consider: How is knowledge produced in the field? Who produces it? Of what is it comprised? Through what media is research in the field typically communicated?

Another exercise can consist of students implementing an informal search of the literature in a discipline by investigating the materials in the local or university library. They can be instructed to browse particular call number ranges of the stacks or compare secondary and tertiary sources related to the field. Another assignment is to ask students to search a particular topic in two related (but discipline-specific) indexes, such as *Sociological Abstracts* (sociology) and *PsycINFO* (psychology), and compare their findings on how two different disciplines approach a given topic and how it is treated in the scholarly research of each particular field.

> **Outcome 1.2.c.** Identifies the value and differences of potential resources in a variety of formats (e.g., multimedia, database, website, data set, audio/visual, book)

> **Outcome 1.2.d.** Identifies the purpose and audience of potential resources (e.g., popular vs. scholarly, current vs. historical)

> **Outcome 1.2.e.** Differentiates between primary and secondary sources, recognizing how their use and importance vary with each discipline

> **Outcome 1.2.f.** Realizes that information may need to be constructed with raw data from primary sources

In research, the nature of the topic determines what formats and types of information are most useful. A knowledgeable student understands that the subject areas covered in his or her research topic will dictate what materials are most suited for the assignment, rather than using only what is familiar and most accessible. Besides varying in level of scholarship, popular and scholarly sources are directed at different audience levels and fill different needs. A student should also be able to recognize the difference between primary and secondary source material and understand that some disciplines rely more heavily on primary source materials than others. Students should realize that both types of sources may have a place in their research.

Assessment Queries

There is an abundance of available assessment queries that address outcomes 1.2.c–f. The following question developed for the *UMBC Survey* broadly addresses outcomes 1.2.c through 1.2.e and targets a student's familiarity with a variety of information sources beyond books and journals. The options contain both less familiar resources (such as dissertations and manuscripts) and more familiar and accessible resources (such as websites and magazines). The following list can be customized to fit the needs of individual institutions.

> Other than "books" and "journals," what other types of information are you familiar with or might you use for a research project/paper? Please select all that apply.
>
>   a. dissertations/theses
>   b. magazines
>   c. newspapers
>   d. websites
>   e. diaries/letters
>   f. manuscripts
>   g. images/pictures
>   h. conference proceedings
>   i. interviews
>   j. television/radio transcripts
>   k. videos/movies/DVDs
>   l. music
>   m. television shows/broadcasts
>   n. radio shows/broadcasts
>   o. speeches
>   p. none of the above
>   q. other: _____

The following question tangentially addresses outcome 1.2.c: "an information-literate student identifies the value and differences of potential resources in a variety of formats." This is an excellent question to include in assessment because it can indicate whether or not students at your institution understand that an online public-access catalog (OPAC) may contain information about books and media items in the library. However, this may not be the case in all libraries.

Typically a library's online catalog contains

  a. information about books, videos, and other nonprint items in the library
  b. the complete text of all the journal articles in the library
  c. information about the college's courses
  d. answers a and b[8]

A number of appropriate questions were identified that address the ability to identify the purpose and audience of potential sources. The following question was accompanied by a table containing descriptions of the three databases that make up the multiple-choice responses.

You want to help your father understand a medical diagnosis. You need to find good information written for the nonexpert. Look at the database descriptions in the box and then select the best source to search for this information need.

  a. NewsBank *NewsFile*
  b. *Health Reference Center–Academic*
  c. *BioMedical Reference Collections: Basic*
  d. Answers a, b, and c

Health Reference Center–Academic, the correct answer, follows the question with the description:

Health Reference Center–Academic

COVERAGE: Articles from a variety of consumer-oriented and professional health periodicals, plus excerpts from health-related reference books. Material includes a medical dictionary; medical directories and reference books; and pamphlets issued by leading health organizations. Updated weekly.[9]

Most libraries have similar descriptions of their subscription databases. Many students find themselves faced with long lists of subject-specific databases after clicking a link such as "Biology and Health Sciences," and they need to be able to determine which database is appropriate for their specific needs. This question reinforces the idea that students need to understand not only the differences between types of sources but also that there are significant subject-related differences among search tools—especially those that are available from the same vendor, such as OCLC *FirstSearch* or EBSCOhost.

There are many ways to assess a student's understanding of the differences between scholarly and popular sources. One way is to use a multiple-choice format like the following, taken from the *Information Literacy Competency Inventory (Maryville Inventory)* at Maryville College in Tennessee.[10]

Which of the following is a characteristic of scholarly journals?

    a. contains glossy pictures and advertisements

    b. reports news events in a timely manner

    c. contains a literature review within the articles

    d. provides an author's opinion about a controversial event

A variation of this type of question, also from the *Maryville Inventory*, is replicated below. Both of these questions can be adjusted for various types of periodicals, such as scholarly, popular, tabloid, trade, and commentary. Both of these questions would benefit from having an "I don't know" option to discourage guessing.

Which of the following titles would be considered the title of a popular magazine?

    a. *Journal of Higher Education*

    b. *Newsweek*

    c. *Economic Review*

    d. *American Journal of Political Science*

Another option is to use the open-ended question format. In this option, students are required or expected to supply their own answers.

Scholarly periodicals like the *American Sociological Review* usually contain very few advertisements. What are two other characteristics of scholarly periodicals?[11]

Information-literate students should be able to identify other characteristics, such as whether a source is written by a scholar or specialist, written in technical or scholarly language, or includes cited references.

A number of questions were identified that assess a student's understanding of the differences between primary and secondary sources.

Which of the following is not a secondary source?

    a. encyclopedia article

    b. letters

    c. newspaper article reporting about a research study

    d. biography[12]

This question includes all secondary source answers except for "letters." The "newspaper" answer is an interesting option to include here because many students are taught that newspapers can be primary sources, and students must think carefully about what it means for a newspaper article to report about a research study or event, rather than provide a first-person account or report data from an original research study. In developing a query for this aspect of Standard 1, it is important to have a clear understanding of what primary and secondary sources mean at your institution and in particular disciplines. In this way, the possibility of confusion over multiple "correct" responses is eliminated.

    Which of the following is a primary source?

    a. a literary text, such as *The Scarlet Letter* by Nathaniel Hawthorne

    b. books written about *The Scarlet Letter*

    c. journal articles written about *The Scarlet Letter*

    d. dissertations written about *The Scarlet Letter*

The correct answer for this question, taken from the *Maryville Inventory*, is "a literary text." This is a challenging question because many students do not think of original literary texts as primary sources. It may not be appropriate for lower-level undergraduates or for those not enrolled in a major that includes an analysis of literary texts. Again, both of the preceding questions would benefit from an "I don't know" option.

    Another approach to assessing the understanding of the concept of primary and secondary sources is to ask students to select the proper definition of one or the other. The first of the next two questions is from the University of California, Berkeley's *History 7B Pretest* (*UC Berkeley Pretest*), and the second is from the instrument used in Lut Rahim Nero's dissertation, *Information Literacy Assessment*. These questions could be adapted to include an assessment of the definitions of secondary and tertiary sources as well.

    A primary source is

      ____ the best source

      ____ a scholarly source

_____ a source created by people involved with or observing
events when they occur

A primary source is

    a. the most important source in your bibliography

    b. the first source you list in your bibliography

    c. a firsthand account: the original source of information

    d. an interpretation of an original source by a foremost expert

The question below, from the *Maryville Inventory*, is a variation of the queries above, providing a method and requiring the student to identify the research type. The "conducting a survey" option could be replaced by other examples of methods of primary research. Additionally, this question would be improved if it included brief definitions, descriptions, or examples of each of the types of research listed in order to avoid confusion and guessing.

Conducting a survey would be an example of

    a. independent research

    b. secondary research

    c. primary research

    d. historical research

Assignments

One way to encourage students to see the value of using a variety of resources in various formats is to have them perform a search on a topic using different types of search tools. For this exercise, depending on the allotted time and the size of the class, it might be helpful to have preselected topics/searches for the students to work with. Students can be instructed to prepare a search statement for an Internet search engine and a database and then to implement the two searches. Students can then examine the results and consider the search strategies they used. This exercise also demonstrates the differences between search tools regarding content and search strategy. For example, a search for "viral meningitis" using www.google.com retrieves pages from the Centers for Disease Control, various fact sheets from health organizations, and a variety of commercial health care sites. The majority of this information is aimed at the consumer, rather than a specialist. Students can compare these results with those found in a database such as *Medline*, which retrieves references to scholarly resources (dissertations, refereed journal articles in a variety of languages, etc.) aimed at the practitioner or researcher. This assignment also demonstrates the importance of selecting the appropriate search tool for your particular information need (2.1).

The ability to identify the purpose and audience of various types of resources is a skill that college-level students need in order to be successful in their research endeavors, but many students struggle with this and have a difficult time distinguishing between scholarly, popular, trade, commentary, and tabloid publications. There are many ways to assist students in learning this skill. By giving students specific criteria for evaluating sources, and teaching them to adopt a healthy amount of skepticism when reading and reviewing information, students can gain a better understanding of the differences between sources. There are many useful library websites that clearly illustrate some of the major differences between publications, such as appearance, audience, content, advertisements, and references. It is useful to discuss these differences with students and to provide them with a copy of a chart or website that details the criteria.[13] (A more in-depth discussion of evaluating criteria can be found in chapter 5.)

Another exercise that encourages students to think about the differences between types of sources is to have them find a bibliographic reference to a study mentioned either in a newspaper or a magazine article, or in the broadcast media (television, radio), and then to locate the study in a scholarly journal. Once they have located the original study, students should then compare the sources of the citation/reference to determine the value and limits of each. A variation of this exercise involves having students read a scholarly article on a topic and a popular article on the same topic and compare the manner in which the two sources deal with the material.

As discussed earlier, students frequently struggle with being able to differentiate between primary and secondary sources and in understanding how their use varies from discipline to discipline. Instructors can use a variety of discipline-specific assignments to teach students about primary resources. Concordia University Libraries has excellent suggestions for assignments that teach these skills.[14] For history students, Patrick Labelle suggests students write a family history as a way to learn about primary sources. Students are encouraged to use primary sources of information such as interviews with family members and public records such as birth and death certificates, marriage licenses, directories, and newspapers. A variation on this exercise can tap into students' creativity and encourage the use of other underused primary sources such as family photo albums and family bibles. Business students can be required to develop a marketing plan for a potential advertising campaign. They will need to identify demographic and financial information, conduct market research, and research product reviews. Students enrolled in English and other writing-intensive courses can be required to write diary entries or the opening chapter of a historical novel, for example, in which they must research the daily routines and customs of people during a particular time period.

ASSESSING KNOWLEDGE OF THE COSTS AND BENEFITS OF ACQUIRING INFORMATION

Performance Indicator 1.3. The information literate student considers the costs and benefits of acquiring the needed information.

> *Outcome 1.3.a*. Determines the availability of needed information and makes decisions on broadening the information seeking process beyond local resources (e.g., interlibrary loan; using resources at other locations; obtaining images, videos, text, or sound)

> *Outcome 1.3.b*. Considers the feasibility of acquiring a new language or skill (e.g., foreign or discipline based) in order to gather needed information and to understand its context

> *Outcome 1.3.c*. Defines a realistic overall plan and timeline to acquire the needed information

One essential component of information literacy is an understanding that the best information for your needs may not be the most handy and accessible. Performance indicator 1.3 highlights the need to be knowledgeable about the acquisition of information. For libraries, the acquisition of materials is usually subject to issues of ownership versus access. Academic—and most other libraries—generally have a combination of print subscriptions and online full-text access through stand-alone subscriptions and online databases. Of course, no one library can own (online or in print) everything, or even a significant portion of all published information. To rectify this, most libraries, even very small ones, have methods of accessing materials that they do not own for their users. Unfortunately, many patrons do not, for various reasons, attempt to use the resources available beyond what is housed in their library's building. Frequently students will seek out only what is immediately available online and in full text. Most libraries do provide their students with interlibrary loan and document delivery services such as Ingenta and Infotrieve, but many students, to the detriment of their research, do not take advantage of these services. Even graduate students are weak in this area. The research literature shows that even if students are aware of these services, some do not give themselves enough time to utilize them. Information-literate students understand that in order to take advantage of the many resources available to them, they need to begin their research early.

For some upper-level students, the need to acquire a particular skill in order to gather needed information or understand its context may arise as they pursue their research. Upper-level history students may need to learn the basics of a foreign language to translate primary source materials. Computer science students may need to become adept at a new programming language in order to fulfill their research or course requirements.

It is important for students to have a realistic plan for acquiring sources and completing their research. This is challenging for students at any educational level. Success in the research process requires a commitment of time and energy on the part of the student.

Assessment Queries

Very few queries were identified for assessing this particular indicator and its accompanying outcomes objectively and independently. However, students can be asked whether or not they are familiar with the services their library provides, or they can be asked to respond to open-ended short-answer questions about their experiences using these services. The following queries were taken from the College of Saint Rose's *Assessment of Information Literacy Skills (Saint Rose Assessment)* and assesses outcome 1.3.a.

Interlibrary loan is a system for Saint Rose students to

    a. purchase books and journals

    b. borrow books owned by the Neil Hellman Library

    c. get books and articles that are not owned by the Neil Hellman Library

    d. travel to area libraries and check books out of them

Which of the following would be the best for identifying any book *not* owned by the Neil Hellman Library?

    a. EBSCOhost *Academic Search*

    b. Modern Language Association (MLA) International Bibliography

    c. Neil Hellman Library Periodicals List

    d. *WorldCat*

The following query was taken from the *FGC Skunk Ape Tutorial* and assesses knowledge of outcomes 1.3.a and c.

What is the most realistic expectation for your library research?

    a. I must realize that I am limited to materials in the FGCU Library or those libraries that I can drive to.

    b. The current catalog is limited and can only search for materials owned by the FGCU Library.

    c. If I want to read older material, I am going to have to use microfilm.

    d. If it does not have what I need, the FGCU Library will get photocopies of materials for me from other libraries.

Assignments

It is clear that many college-level students do not use resources beyond what is housed in their academic libraries. Though some students have discovered the value of using interlibrary loan services, many others are unfamiliar with the process of ordering material owned by another institution. It is useful to show students how to order something through the service and then require them to use the service at least once so they can become familiar with the process. One useful exercise is to have students locate a book or journal article not owned by their home institution and then request the item through ILL. Students should write a short summary of how they identified the book or article; they should include a citation of the item and provide a short evaluation of the service. This assignment is best used in conjunction with a larger research project, such as a paper or presentation. Students should request items they can use for that project in order to make the assignment purposeful, useful, and economical for the student as well as the institution.

Some institutions may charge students for ILL services. For this type of assignment, students need to have a basic understanding of the library catalog and must be able to use it to see which periodicals and other materials are owned by their institutions and which are not.

ASSESSING THE ABILITY TO REEVALUATE ONE'S INFORMATION NEED

Performance Indicator 1.4. The information literate student reevaluates the nature and extent of the information need.

> ***Outcome 1.4.a***. Reviews the initial information need to clarify, revise, or refine the question

> ***Outcome 1.4.b***. Describes criteria used to make information decisions and choices

Knowledgeable students recognize that they may need to revise their original topic and research questions if they find that the resources they have identified are insufficient. A student may also realize that an assessment of the gathered information shows an error or disconnect in thinking regarding the original research questions. To do this, students need to be able to retrace their steps in the research process in order to reevaluate the original nature and extent of the information need. This may involve revising the original outline, if necessary, and clarifying and refining the original research question. Unfortunately, these are steps that are frequently overlooked or not performed by time-pressed students.

Assessment Query

One way to assess the last indicator of this standard is to ask students how frequently they do certain tasks related to revising and reevaluating their information needs. The following question from the *UMBC Survey* asks students to specify how often they do each task. Students responded using a Likert-type scale comprised of the following: very frequently, frequently, occasionally, infrequently, or never.

> After you have done your initial research for a paper, how often do you do the following?

    a. Understand all of the information.

    b. Discuss findings with friends and colleagues.

    c. Make an outline.

    d. Review the original research question to determine if additional information is needed.

    e. Discard irrelevant or useless findings.

    f. Look at material under each outline heading and synthesize major points and concepts.

NOTES

1. Bay Area Community Colleges Assessment Project Team, *Bay Area Community Colleges Assessment Project: A Two-Part Information Competency Assessment Exam*, http://www.topsy.org/ICAP/ICAProject.html. The Bay Area Community Colleges Assessment Project Team includes Bonnie Gratch-Lindauer, project leader, Pam Baker, Amelie Brown, Micca Gray, Andy Kivel, Brian Lym, and Topsy Smalley.

2. Bay Area Assessment Team, *Bay Area Community Colleges Assessment Project*.

3. Ibid.

4. Carol C. Kuhlthau, "Inside the Search Process: Information Seeking from the User's Perspective," *Journal of the American Society for Information Science* 42 (1991): 369.

5. Judy Swanson, California Polytechnic State University, San Luis Obispo, "CSU Information Competence: Please Select a Tutorial . . . Define the Research Topic," http://www.lib.calpoly.edu/infocomp/modules/.

6. Claudia J. Morner, "A Test of Library Research Skills for Education Doctoral Students" (Ph.D. diss., Boston College, 1993), 149.

7. Teresa Y. Neely, *Sociological and Psychological Aspects of Information Literacy in Higher Education* (Lanham, MD: Scarecrow, 2002), 119.

8. Bay Area Assessment Team, *Bay Area Community Colleges Assessment Project*.

9. Ibid.

10. This survey instrument was produced by Roger Myers of Maryville College, Tennessee. It was part of a presentation by Christine Nugent, of Warren Wilson College, at the Association of College and Research Libraries' 11th National Conference, "Learning to Make a Difference," Charlotte, NC, April 10–13, 2003. See http://www.warren-wilson.edu/~library/acrl.htm.

11. Bay Area Assessment Team, *Bay Area Community Colleges Assessment Project*.

12. Ibid.

13. See Humboldt State University Library, "Journals—Scholarly or Popular?" http://library.humboldt.edu/infoservices/scholorpop.htm.

14. Patrick R. Labelle, Concordia University Libraries, "Designing Meaningful Library Assignments—Writing a Family History," http://library.concordia.ca/services/users/faculty/assignment.html.

Accessing Information Effectively and Efficiently

Teresa Y. Neely

STANDARD 2
The information literate student assesses needed
information effectively and efficiently.

Standard 2 covers a significant range of research-related activities, including selecting a methodology, searching techniques, and retrieving and managing information. This chapter will provide examples of assessment questions developed to evaluate students' competency with this standard and will also describe some assignments that can be used to improve students' proficiency for this standard.

Standard 2 is one of the most detailed standards, with five performance indicators and twenty-two accompanying outcomes. It is critical for college-level students to be able to access the information they need to complete assignments and other course requirements effectively and efficiently. The majority of college-level students have little trouble finding data. The problems arise when they are required to select appropriate investigative methodologies for their research tasks (2.1.a); design and implement effective search strategies (2.2); retrieve information using a variety of methods (2.3); and extract, record, and manage the information they find (2.5). The literature of library and information science and higher education reveals that these are tasks that students are either unfamiliar with or are unequipped to complete adequately.[1]

Standard 2 is also the stage where a lack of knowledge about available discipline-specific resources becomes most evident. If students do not know where to look for appropriate resources, then they are operating at an information deficit from the beginning of the research process. Faculty and librarians play a key role in helping students to identify appropriate resources for their research projects by making recommendations and suggestions for resources including, but not limited to, key print reference sources, subject-related databases, and professional, state, and federal websites.

ASSESSING THE ABILITY TO SELECT A RESEARCH METHODOLOGY

Performance Indicator 2.1. The information literate student selects the most appropriate investigative methods or information retrieval systems for accessing the needed information.

> ***Outcome 2.1.a.*** Identifies appropriate investigative methods (e.g., laboratory experiment, simulation, fieldwork)
>
> ***Outcome 2.1.b.*** Investigates benefits and applicability of various investigative methods
>
> ***Outcome 2.1.c.*** Investigates the scope, content, and organization of information retrieval systems
>
> ***Outcome 2.1.d.*** Selects efficient and effective approaches for accessing the information needed from the investigative method or information retrieval system

In terms of library research, the first performance indicator for this standard addresses the ability to select a database or information resource. This means that students should be able to decide what research methodology (laboratory experiment, simulation fieldwork, survey, focus group, library research) they should use to satisfy their research task. In making this decision, it is inherently presumed that students include in their investigation an analysis of the benefits and applicability of the research methodology chosen. They should ask questions like: What is my research question or information need?

Which methodology will get me the information I need to complete this assignment? For most college-level students, the research methodology is determined by the assignment, which in turn is usually determined by the teaching faculty; however, in some cases, students enrolled in graduate programs or in the sciences or engineering may have more flexibility in the selection of a methodology.

It is important to note that although the standards address a broad range of information literacy skills, there are some steps that are not explicitly addressed. For example, the fact that a student is at the stage to select an information retrieval system presupposes that the student is familiar with the systems in his or her subject area. Most students, especially lower-level undergraduates, have not been exposed to subject databases, however. Too many students turn to the Internet, and too few turn to reference books and materials during the research process. In addition, limited research on faculty-student interaction reveals that faculty do not always model positive information-literate behavior.[2]

Assessment Queries

The *UMBC Survey* includes several questions appropriate for outcome 2.1.a. One query provides students with a list of seven items, including an option for "other," and asks them, "Where do you go to find information?" In addition to options for asking friends, professors, teaching assistants, or graduate assistants, options for "use Internet search engine," "go to the library web page," "use faculty course website," and "go to the library" are also included. This type of question presumes very little about students' prior subject or general database knowledge. In an effort to discern information-seeking behavior, it asks where they go if they have an information need.

A follow-up question from the *UMBC Survey* gives students an opportunity to respond to how they find information sources once they are given a particular research topic. Again, an "other" option is included in the list of twelve types of resources, which include people (librarians, friends, faculty); print resources (encyclopedias, abstracts and indexes, newspaper archives); online (Internet, abstracts and indexes [databases]); and other types of resources (television/radio transcripts, radio news, television news).

In trying to understand the nature of self-reported levels of competencies, the Rappahannock Community College (Virginia), in its *Information Literacy Assessment*, uses this type of query to its advantage. Students are asked to indicate which information sources/services they used to complete their assignments, using a list of seventeen items, including an "Other" category with a free text option. This question also provides data on the information-seeking process on whether students select appropriate resources to search for their topics. A follow-up question provides an excellent way to find out how the students decided which index or database to use.

> How did you decide which indexes/databases to use?
>
> ____ I used the library research guide on the RCC library web page
>
> ____ Suggestion by librarian
>
> ____ Suggestion by instructor
>
> ____ Suggestion by classmate or friend
>
> ____ Other, please specify _____

This question reveals so much more than what it actually asks for. It tells whether the student has consulted a librarian for assistance; whether or not the course instructor is modeling positive information-literate behavior by making suggestions about resources; whether the library's website and research guides are being used; and if the student is relying on friends and colleagues instead of authoritative guidance in making decisions about information retrieval systems.

Patricia Daragan and Gwendolyn Stevens developed and implemented several versions of the *Coast Guard Academy Library Research Skills Assessment* (*CGA Skills Assessment*) at the U.S. Coast Guard Academy.[3] The following query, from the 1996 edition, is one of nineteen that were included in the *CGA Skills Assessment*. These items could be adapted to assess other subject-specific database competencies.

> The questions in this section assess your knowledge of the various information resources available in an academic library. Write, on the line provided, the letter which corresponds to the best answer.
>
> ____ Citations to, and abstracts of, articles about bilingual education
>
> a. *Resources in Education*
>
> b. *Humanities Index*
>
> c. *P.A.I.S.*

Theoretically, this is a good method to assess students' ability to select an appropriate information retrieval system (2.1.a.), but given the wide range of subject areas covered in the original instrument, the inclusion of a variety of topics may not be appropriate for your audience. The authors note that freshmen cadets take a variety of courses: calculus, English composition and literature, chemistry, organizational behavior, nautical science, introduction to engineering and computers, and academic orientation study skills.[4] Bibliographic instruction is also integrated in the first-year component, but most undergraduates elsewhere do not have the advantage of being exposed to broad subject areas during their first year. It is recommended that when using this type of query, for this particular performance indicator (2.1), all of the questions should be written for a single academic discipline or should be general in nature.

This type of query can also be used to determine what students know about the makeup of other types of sources. The University of Washington's *Information Literacy* (*General Studies 391*) questionnaire (*UW Information Literacy* questionnaire) includes the following question:

> A class you are taking requires that you read three journal articles related to a topic of your choosing. Which of the following would be the best tool to use in order to obtain a list of journal articles for your topic?
>
> _____ an online library catalog (e.g., UW Online Catalog)
>
> _____ an index (e.g., *Expanded Academic Index*)
>
> _____ an encyclopedia

This question uses a scenario with which the student is probably familiar and determines whether he or she knows that journal articles can be obtained from an index. It is also written from the student's perspective and is not discipline-specific.

Berea College's *Bibliographic Instruction Program Evaluation* (*Berea College Evaluation*) includes two questions appropriate for performance indicators 2.1.b and c. The options can easily be revised depending upon how you refer to resources and sources in your library (e.g., "card catalog" vs. "online public-access catalog [OPAC]"). One question requires students to determine the most appropriate place in the library to search for information. The places listed to choose from are:

book stacks   card catalog

circulation desk	reference area
current periodicals	reserve desk
index area	serial record
microfilm area	special collections

A sample of the information items to search for includes:

____ to find out if the library has the *Journal of American History* for 1972

____ articles on diet and exercise published in the last two or three years

____ the most recent issues of magazines to browse

____ 1955 newspaper on film

____ addresses of members of Congress

This question, for the most part, will allow you to determine immediately if students know which source they need to use to find the answer to the questions. However, the following items that were also included may be confusing or misleading:

____ recent census data on Calloway County, Kentucky

____ journal literature on participation of Blacks in World War II

It might be beneficial to list parts of the reference area such as "government documents" so that students would know where to find census data, or to list the years for World War II so students would know whether to look in the "index area," the "microfilm area," or "current periodicals."

A second question from the same instrument asks students to determine which type of resources would be the most appropriate to consult for the information item described. This question relates to performance indicators 2.1.b and c and assesses students' understanding of the applicability, scope, content, and organization of various types of information retrieval systems. The types of resources listed include:

almanac	dictionary
bibliography	encyclopedia
biographical dictionary	newspaper index
card catalog	periodical index
computer databases	statistical handbook

A sample of the information items described includes:

    ____ magazine article on gun control

    ____ titles of books written by Willa Cather available in Hutchins Library

    ____ birthday of Tina Turner

    ____ day-by-day accounts of the Oliver North trial

    ____ names of all Nobel Peace Prize winners since 1901

    ____ mailing address of Tom Hanks

It is important to remember when writing information items such as these that the subject matter should be appropriate for a particular discipline (education, psychology) or a particular group of students (freshmen, graduate students). Writing items that require or appear to require prior knowledge or subject expertise may be confusing and lead a student to focus more on the subject of the question than on the actual selection of the correct item. For example, other items from the *Berea College Evaluation* for this question are:

    ____ A brief overview, with a bibliography, on the economic history of agriculture in the South

    ____ A source that, by rapidly combining the subjects on in vitro fertilization, medical ethics, and legal issues, will provide access to a large number of journal articles published since 1983

It can be assumed that the answer to the first item is "encyclopedia," and the answer to the second one is "computer databases" and not "periodical index," but will an undergraduate student be able to make the same assumption? There is an inherent danger in including too much subject-specific information in the question that may not be necessary to get the response you desire.

Also, keep in mind the context for assessment. It is unknown how this particular survey instrument was administered at Berea College, but it might be helpful to use this type of question with students who have completed a tour, orientation, or virtual tour of the library, or in conjunction with a well-designed self-paced tour.

Regarding outcome 2.1.c, Lut Rahim Nero and Claudia J. Morner included appropriate queries in instruments developed or used in their dissertations. Nero's 1999 dissertation used the *Information Literacy Assessment* instrument and included a question to assess students' knowledge of the scope of subject databases and general periodical indexes:

> In comparing a subject periodicals index to a general periodical index, only the subject index
>
> a. is broader in scope, cites more magazine articles
> b. has more in-depth subject coverage, cites more journal articles
> c. should be used to find popular-interest periodicals
> d. includes "see" and "see also" references

A recommended revision to this question could be made so that the stem reads more positively: "Which of the following is true of the subject index?" Findings for this question reveal whether students are familiar with, or aware of, the difference between general and subject periodical indexes.

Morner's 1993 dissertation produced the *Morner Test* and included the following:

> Articles and documents in *ERIC* are
>
> a. carefully screened to reflect the best of education literature
> b. from a wide range of sources
> c. international, encompassing the world's education literature
> d. primarily scholarly reports of education research

The *Morner Test* assessed Ph.D. students in education, but this question could be revised to assess the awareness of the scope of any discipline-based or general database, local online catalog, or union catalog.

Assignments

A variety of assignments were identified to assist students in the acquisition of skills to select the most appropriate resources and databases in order to do their research; however, the majority of these required students to select an appropriate database for a list of unrelated research topics. The original assignment below listed more than one question.

> Choose the *best* database to answer [each of] the questions below. Write the database name below the question with a one-sentence explanation as to why you chose that database.
>
> You are getting ready to interview for a job with Nike. You don't know anything about the company or the sporting goods industry.

> Name a database you could use to find articles about the company
> and the industry so you don't look stupid during the interview.[5]

Students are instructed to not use *Academic Search*, but the assignment does
not appear to include a description of the databases so that students can
make informed choices. (See chapter 3 for examples of queries with database
descriptions.) Assignments such as these do not take into consideration that
the student may not know which database to select initially. There are hun-
dreds of databases, subject-specific and multidisciplinary, and students need
to be given instruction in and exposure to appropriate subject databases before they can be required to select which database might be most appropriate
for identifying resources on topics unrelated to their major or department.

An assignment for freshmen music students at Virginia Commonwealth
University requires students to research one of the National Public Radio top
100 songs. Students must determine if the library owns the recording or
score, and if not, they must locate a related recording or score. In addition,
they must also find a related magazine or journal article and a related entry
from the library's reference collection. Jimmy Ghaphery, the creator of the
assignment, notes, "We have found that this is an engaging way to introduce
these students to print and online research options as well as giving them an
understanding of the strengths and weakness of our music collection."[6]

Another assignment appropriate for this performance indicator requires
students to write a critique of various databases in a particular discipline, including their coverage, design, and search interface.

ASSESSING THE ABILITY TO DEVELOP
SEARCH STRATEGIES

Performance Indicator 2.2. The information literate student constructs
and implements effectively designed search strategies.

> *Outcome 2.2.a*. Develops a research plan appropriate to the
> investigative method
>
> *Outcome 2.2.b*. Identifies keywords, synonyms, and related
> terms for the information needed
>
> *Outcome 2.2.c*. Selects controlled vocabulary specific to the
> discipline or information retrieval source

Once an appropriate information retrieval system has been selected, and its scope, content, and organization have been analyzed, information-literate students "construct and implement successful search strategies." While identifying appropriate resources is vital in connecting students with the information they need, developing a proper search strategy is equally as important. There is empirical evidence that college-level students do not possess the ability to access the information they need to complete course assignment requirements. Moreover, the self-reported attitudes of college-level students about developing successful search strategies reveal that they often overestimate their abilities.[7]

Controlled Vocabulary

Before a student begins searching, it is always a good idea to identify "keywords, synonyms, and related terms for the information needed." Research shows that students are often unfamiliar with how databases and library catalogs are constructed, indexed, and organized.[8] In order to obtain the most relevant search results, students must use the terminology that is used to index documents and resources in the database or library catalog. For most databases, these lists of words, called controlled vocabulary, are usually available in the form of a thesaurus or descriptor list; and for library catalogs, major cataloging schemes are the norm: Library of Congress classification system, Dewey decimal classification system. Browsing these lists, online or in print, can provide the student with the most appropriate search terms to use.

Natural Language Searching

In addition to controlled vocabulary, there are other ways that students tend to search. Many students will type in an entire sentence or fragment of a sentence hoping to obtain relevant results. This is known as natural language searching. This sort of searching is most effective in a full-text database or in generally searching the Internet; however, students often use this method with systems that do not operate using natural language searching. Full-text databases usually allow searching in all fields and throughout the text. In other words, you are not limited to searching in a particular field such as title, author, descriptors, and so on. *LexisNexis*, *EthnicNewswatch*, and *Electric Library* are three such databases that are primarily full text. When searching in a database that contains links to the full text of journal articles, this option to search the full text may or may not be available, as searching may be limited to particular fields.

Assessment Queries

The *Information Competency Assessment* at California State Polytechnic University, Pomona (*Cal Poly–Pomona Information Competency Assessment*), includes several questions that provide a research topic or question and then ask students to determine the key concepts in the statement (2.2.b.). Queries such as these assist students in learning how to take a research topic and determine which words will be the most effective when searching for information. It also represents a natural progression from Standard 1 (recognizing and articulating a need) to Standard 2 (accessing the information needed).

What are the key concepts of the following statement? "Discuss how the breakup of the Soviet Union has impacted U.S. foreign policy."

____   Breakup, foreign policy, U.S., Soviet Union

____   Soviet Union, U.S.

____   U.S. foreign policy, Soviet Union foreign policy

In terms of outcome 2.2.c, there are a number of assessment queries that can be developed to assess students' knowledge of controlled vocabulary. The *Neely Test* adapted this next item from the *Morner Test*.

When selecting subject terms from an online catalog, which of the following would you use terms from?

a. *Dictionary of Education*

b. *Thesaurus of ERIC Descriptors*

c. Library of Congress Subject Headings

d. Prior reading

e. I don't know

Although this question was initially written for education students, the first two options can easily be revised for a more general query or for another discipline. One method for determining whether students are familiar with or aware of controlled vocabulary is to simply ask them. One *UMBC Survey* question on the frequency of use of searching techniques, described below under "Searching Techniques," included "controlled vocabulary" as one of the options. A question such as this does not ask respondents to comment on their expertise or skill set; it simply asks them to tell you how often they use it. Responses to this inquiry could provide valuable information on whether or not students are familiar with the concept of controlled vocabulary.

>*Outcome 2.2.d.* Constructs a search strategy using appropriate commands for the information retrieval system selected (e.g., Boolean operators, truncation, and proximity for search engines; internal organizers such as indexes for books)

>*Outcome 2.2.e.* Implements the search strategy in various information retrieval systems using different user interfaces and search engines, with different command languages, protocols, and search parameters

>*Outcome 2.2.f.* Implements the search using investigative protocols appropriate to the discipline

Searching Techniques

Developing successful search strategies requires a student to be familiar with information retrieval systems and to have the ability to select one that is appropriate for his or her research needs. In most cases, students will have already been exposed to at least one information retrieval system from a vendor that provides access to many; for example, EBSCO or OCLC *FirstSearch*. In these cases, searching methods and techniques are usually transferable. However, in general, the methods for using searching techniques such as proximity searching, Boolean operators, or truncation vary greatly from database to database and also in library catalogs.

The *UMBC Survey* contains a question that lists a number of searching techniques: truncation; Boolean "and," "or," and "not"; limiters; proximity operators; cross- and multiple-field searching; and use of controlled vocabulary. Each technique is accompanied by an example to further illustrate the concept. Students are asked to indicate, using a Likert-type scale, the frequency with which they have used the various techniques. Although this question solicits self-reported data, it does not require students to guess what the techniques are, for example, limiters (limit search by date, publisher, language, type of material), nor does it require them to indicate their proficiency;

rather, it asks how often they have used the technique when conducting research in electronic databases.

Another question from the *Cal Poly–Pomona Information Competency Assessment* asks students: "Which of the following statements will get the best information from a database search on this topic?" The topics are examples of questions that determine whether or not students are familiar with Boolean logic. The question also assesses their ability to select appropriate keywords, given a topic, that will yield relevant resources.

"Discuss capital punishment as a deterrent to crime."

____ Capital Punishment OR Crime

____ Deterrent AND Crime

____ Capital Punishment AND Crime

"Describe the characteristics of an asthma or hay fever attack."

____ Asthma AND Hay Fever

____ Asthma OR Hay Fever

____ Characteristics AND Attack

With regard to assessing students' use of other searching techniques, the *Neely Test* adapted the following queries on Boolean operators and truncation from the *Morner Test*.

What is your next logical step when your search yields 2,000 citations?

    a. Add another term to the search using "and" command.

    b. Add another term to the search using "or" command.

    c. Look at all of them in order to be thorough.

    d. Look at the first few.

    e. I don't know.

"Truncation" is a library computer-searching term meaning that the last letter or letters of a word [are] substituted with a symbol, such as "*" or "\$". A good reason you might truncate a search term such as child* is that truncation will

    a. limit search to descriptor or subject heading field

    b. reduce the number of irrelevant citations

    c. save searcher typing time

  d. yield more citations

  e. I don't know

The latter question is particularly well written in that the student does not have to guess at what truncation is. The student is provided with a description of the concept and then given options for using it.

Assignments

With the exception of Standard 3 (evaluating information), this performance indicator (2.2) is probably the easiest to develop assignments for. With concrete, measurable outcomes such as controlled vocabulary; keywords, synonyms, and related terms; and numerous search strategy options, there are many good assignment examples to choose from.

  Kimberly E. Kelley at the University of Maryland University College (UMUC) describes an assignment in which students are asked to "develop a plan to retrieve information in a variety of formats, evaluate the located information, cite their sources appropriately, and present their findings to class."[9] Although there is only limited published evidence on the use of journal logs for information-seeking purposes by college-level students, this methodology fits when used as an assignment that assists students in developing successful search strategies. Librarians at the Memorial University of Newfoundland Libraries propose that the development of successful search strategies can be enhanced when students keep logs or journals of research steps taken and note the relevance of their results.[10]

  Kristin Johnson at California State University, Chico, has developed an assignment in which students use the Library of Congress Subject Headings (LCSH).[11] Students are asked to identify, off the top of their heads, a topic for their major or a subject area of interest. They also have to write down two additional related terms that either broaden or narrow their topic. The next step is to complete a table that requires them to consult the LCSH to determine if their term is present, whether it is an official term, and if not, whether they were referred to the official term. If they were referred to an official heading, they are required to fill out the form accordingly. Students are then required to identify and write down the Library of Congress classification number (if any) and to note and write down any related LCSHs above or below their heading. This assignment illuminates the connection between the subject classification scheme and the call number used to locate the materials on the shelf, thereby satisfying performance indicator 2.3 (retrieving information) as well.

A librarian from New Mexico State University has developed an assignment that addresses how subject headings change over time.[12] Students are instructed to select a current topic that has been around for the past fifty years or so. Examples of the guidelines given for topic selection include:

> *Communicable diseases* have been around for a long time
>   but *AIDS* has not.

> *Space travel* has been written about for centuries but the
>   *space shuttle* is a recent invention.

> *War* has been around since Homer was a pup but the *Persian
>   Gulf War* is a fairly recent event.

After topic selection, students are instructed to locate and record the subject headings using the last five years of the *Readers' Guide to Periodical Literature*. Students are then required to repeat this exercise, using the same topic in another index. Finally, students are instructed to use the same topic and identify subject headings that represent relevant items using issues of the *Readers' Guide to Periodical Literature* published prior to 1950.

The basis for an assignment from Weber State University (Utah) promotes the use of controlled vocabulary.[13] This assignment teaches students that using different databases may require the use of different terminology to search for resources on the same topic. Students could be assigned several databases, including the library's catalog, and asked to identify and record the appropriate terms for a particular topic in all of them. This assignment works well when historical and out-of-date terms for race, ethnicity, and sexual orientation are used.[14] Depending on the assignment, whether historical or contemporary, students will be introduced to the concepts of controlled vocabularies, descriptors, subject headings, keywords, and thesauri.

Concept mapping, to teach students how to break down a research topic into key components and then explore that topic (discussed and illustrated in chapter 3), is advocated by librarians at Central Queensland University, Australia, and at the State University of New York, Geneseo.[15] Librarians at Central Queensland University approach this assignment by requiring students to select a topic from a list of common everyday terms. Students then develop a concept map or search strategy that is appropriate for searching databases, the library catalog, and the Internet for each term.

Another assignment from Central Queensland University requires students to paraphrase what they have learned about search strategies for a younger sister or brother who has asked for their help on a school assignment.[16] This assignment requires students to have mastered the nature of search strategies and the ability to communicate them in plain English, or layman's terms, for a younger student. This particular assignment is not recommended for lower-level undergraduates, but for students who have been exposed to search strategies and have used and reinforced these skills over time, it would be ideal.

Another assignment requires students to write the headline for a preselected paragraph from which all identifying information has been stripped. The students then share what they have written and compare it to the actual headline for the paragraph. An interactive discussion is held when the librarian or instructor picks key words from the paragraph and asks how many headlines contained those key words, then points out how many did not. A similarly effective activity is distributing paint chips in varying shades of one color, for example, blue. The interactive discussion could then include the creative names for the shades of blue and how many different ways you can say *blue* to sell paint, and also how many of the chips actually contain the word *blue*.

ASSESSING THE ABILITY TO RETRIEVE INFORMATION

Performance Indicator 2.3. The information literate student retrieves information online or in person using a variety of methods.

> *Outcome 2.3.a.* Uses various search systems to retrieve information in a variety of formats
>
> *Outcome 2.3.b.* Uses various classification schemes and other systems (e.g., call number systems or indexes) to locate information resources within the library or to identify specific sites for physical exploration

The ACRL Standards do not explicitly address what students do after they access information and before they retrieve it. There is evidence that along with a deficit of searching skills themselves, college-level students do not know what they have identified and thus do not know how to retrieve it. This is a critical step, because if students don't know what the list of citations they have retrieved represents, they could waste valuable time looking for a book in a database, or searching a catalog using the journal article's title instead of the title of the journal itself. A careful review of the database record, specifically the field names (e.g., Title, Author, Source), can reveal valuable information about the bibliographic citation. But students are often unable to discern that Source means the source of the article, as in the journal title. When it comes to published bibliographies, and course syllabi with reference listings, where there are no field names, students are often not familiar with citation styles, and since these can be so varied—some italicize the title of journal, others underline, and so on—this makes it even more difficult to figure out just what they are looking for.

There is a general consensus among students and other library users that federated searching, or the ability to search multiple library resources simultaneously, is a good thing. This creates a dilemma for librarians, because the potential for increased frustration and confusion for the user is multiplied once results lists contain a multitude of resources in a variety of formats from various types of sources. Databases such as *PsycINFO* are ahead of the game with citations assigned to one of eight types of sources (authored book, edited book, chapter, journal, peer-reviewed journal, dissertation abstract, report, secondary publication). The examples below are *PsycINFO* citations for a book chapter and a peer-reviewed journal article.

> Coronary heart disease and hypertension. O'Callahan, Mark; Andrews, Amy M.; Krantz, David S.; In: *Handbook of psychology: Health psychology*, Vol. 9. Nezu, Arthur M.; Nezu, Christine Maguth; New York, NY, US: John Wiley & Sons, Inc, 2003. pp. 339–364. [Chapter]

> Awareness, treatment, and control of vascular risk factors in African Americans with stroke. Ruland, S.; Raman, R.; Chaturvedi, S.; *Neurology*, Vol 60(1), Jan 2003. pp. 64–68. [Peer Reviewed Journal]

This kind of added value to abstracting and indexing sources is ideal but far from universal. Some vendors, such as OCLC *FirstSearch* and EBSCO, allow users to search more than one database at a time. Libraries are also increasingly moving toward providing seamless off-campus access to electronic resources, including the catalog, and full-text e-journals through portals. This is a good thing in that it allows users to search multiple electronic resources simultaneously, but retrieving materials based on the citations resulting from such a search will continue to be problematic as long as students do not have the expertise to identify what the citations represent.

In addition, students need to be familiar with how libraries and information are organized. They need to understand classification systems such as the Library of Congress classification scheme and the Superintendent of Documents classification scheme, among others, in order to find resources organized and housed in libraries or available electronically. They need to understand the difference between reference, stacks, and government documents in order to determine where to go in libraries to find information, and the difference between the library catalog, databases, and indexes. They also need to understand the concept of access versus ownership, when libraries, due to a variety of circumstances, focus their efforts on providing access to information rather than acquiring it and storing it physically in the library.

Assessment Queries

The *UMBC Survey* includes two questions for this performance indicator. One question provides a citation from a journal with the major elements numbered and asks students to match the numbered items to a list of citation elements. A related question provides a list of citation types and asks students to decide what each citation represents. This type of assessment query can also be used to discern primary sources from secondary sources (see outcome 1.2.d).

> ***Outcome 2.3.c.*** Uses specialized online or in-person services available at the institution to retrieve information needed (e.g., interlibrary loan/document delivery, professional associations, institutional research offices, community resources, experts, and practitioners)

> ***Outcome 2.3.d.*** Uses surveys, letters, interviews, and other forms of inquiry to retrieve primary information

There is empirical evidence that although graduate students are aware of available library services, they still perceive the need for bibliographic instruction.[17] All students should be familiar with library services like interlibrary loan, cooperative resource-sharing agreements (which may allow them privileges to use and check out materials from other libraries in a consortium), and document delivery (wherein the library provides access via certain vendors to full-text documents delivered on demand via fax or electronically). In times of extreme budget constraints coupled with escalating serials costs and serials cancellation projects, it is not realistic for any one library to attempt to physically acquire everything. Students need to be aware of the circumstances and the variety of options available to them to access and retrieve information. Depending on the student's level and the research need, it may be necessary to use a variety of formats to retrieve primary source information. Students completing research projects for dissertations, theses, and senior research projects may choose to gather data using surveys, letters, interviews, and other methods of inquiry. The use of these research methods is usually determined earlier in this standard (2.1.a, 2.1.d), but students should be aware of the possibilities and also of the responsibilities of using such methods.

Assessment Queries

In order to determine if students are familiar with services offered in many libraries, Anne C. Moore's 2001 dissertation uses the *New Mexico State University Information Literacy Instrument* to ask the following:

> The service offered in most public and academic libraries that allows you to get almost any publication you need is called
>
> a. reserves
> b. reference
> c. interlibrary loan
> d. full text

A more specific question about interlibrary loan service was developed by Morner for the *Morner Test*:

> Which of the following *best* describes how to locate dissertations from other schools? They are available
>
> a. at no cost from University Microfilm
> b. on computer in full-text format
> c. on microfiche at many university libraries
> d. through interlibrary loan

This question could easily be revised to make it more general. Students could be asked to pick the statement that describes how to locate journal articles or books from other schools. They could also be asked to respond to queries about the availability and use of other services that your library offers. A key aspect in the acquisition and use of information literacy skills is transferability. It is a good idea to keep in mind that the students you are assessing may not spend their entire academic career at your institution. Resist the temptation to write questions that are too focused on your institution's individual practices and procedures. For example, all institutions do not charge for ILL, but some do. In terms of local quizzes and one-shot lectures, it may be appropriate to quiz students at this level of granularity on ILL practices; however, in terms of information literacy assessment, this approach may not be the ideal.

Assignments

Richard Feinberg at the State University of New York, Stony Brook, describes an assignment where students are required to analyze a bibliography of sources, identify what the citations represent, and then determine whether the local library owns them.[18] Before students can locate resources, they must be able to determine what that resource is. This is an excellent assignment in developing this skill, and moreover it goes a step further and illustrates outcome 2.3.b. Once students have determined whether a citation represents a book, a book chapter, a journal, or a dissertation, they need the skills to be able to find it. If it is a book, then they need to know that the next step is the library's catalog; if it is a book chapter, they need to know that the next step is the library's catalog, but to search for the book title and not the chapter title.

Joan Reitz, instruction librarian at Western Connecticut State University, has developed an interactive Library of Congress call number quiz.[19] It is designed to teach students basic call number order skills. A similar quiz could be designed to teach students the Superintendent of Documents classification scheme or a local classification scheme developed for a special collection or for local/state government documents.

Librarians at Central Queensland University describe an assignment that challenges students to find alternatives to texts and resources recommended by teaching faculty.[20] Working in small groups, students can identify a range of strategies such as requesting materials via ILL or cooperative resource-sharing agreements, selecting an earlier edition of the same text, or browsing the shelves in the same call number area.

ASSESSING THE ABILITY TO REFINE SEARCH STRATEGIES

Performance Indicator 2.4. The information literate student refines the search strategy if necessary.

> ***Outcome 2.4.a.*** Assesses the quantity, quality, and relevance of the search results to determine whether alternative information retrieval systems or investigative methods should be utilized

> ***Outcome 2.4.b.*** Identifies gaps in the information retrieved and determines if the search strategy should be revised

> ***Outcome 2.4.c.*** Repeats the search using the revised strategy as necessary

Very few queries or assignments of quality were identified for this particular performance indicator. This is a stage where students often become frustrated, and unfortunately, anecdotal evidence reveals that they receive very little guidance from faculty, with the exception of the comment, "You need more scholarly/academic sources." Students often spend a great deal of time searching for and retrieving materials that turn out to be inappropriate or outside the scope of their research topic. Developing assignments that build on each other and providing frequent feedback would eliminate the scenario that often occurs at the reference desk, whereby the student has already completed the term paper or research project, but the professor has informed them that they "just need one or two more journal articles for the bibliography."

Assessment Query

The *UMBC Survey* includes one question that asks students about their actions after completing their initial research. Students are asked to indicate the frequency with which they complete certain tasks. Of interest to outcomes 2.4.b and c are the following statements from this question:

a. understand all of the information

b. discuss findings with friends and colleagues

c. review the original research questions to determine if additional information is needed

   d. discard irrelevant or useless information

   e. revise outline based on research findings

Responses to these statements can provide researchers with key information about what students do with all the information they have gathered. Far too frequently, students begin the gathering process prior to refining the actual research topic. When this occurs, students have searched information retrieval systems, printed out articles, and checked out books but are still not clear on the focus of the topic itself.

Assignment

An assignment developed by Sue Ann Brainard at the State University of New York, Geneseo, describes a scenario for students who have been exposed to databases but are not proficient at refining search strategies. Students are given a search topic along with a failed first search attempt and then told why the search was not successful. They are then asked to refine the search statement until they get satisfactory results.[21] This assignment teaches troubleshooting skills and also enhances and reinforces critical thinking skills.

ASSESSING THE ABILITY TO MANAGE INFORMATION

Performance Indicator 2.5. The information literate student extracts, records, and manages the information and its sources.

> ***Outcome 2.5.a***. Selects among various technologies the most appropriate one for the task of extracting the needed information (e.g., copy/paste software functions, photocopier, scanner, audio/visual equipment, or exploratory instruments)

> ***Outcome 2.5.b***. Creates a system for organizing the information

> ***Outcome 2.5.c***. Differentiates between the types of sources cited and understands the elements and correct syntax of a citation for a wide range of resources

> ***Outcome 2.5.d***. Records all pertinent citation information for future reference

Outcome 2.5.e. Uses various technologies to manage the information selected and organized

Although there is no obvious justification for it, this performance indicator appears to be the most problematic one for college-level students; if not the most problematic, then definitely the most overlooked. It is the equivalent of the bread crumbs used by Hansel and Gretel to find their way back home. Students often do not understand the importance of recording complete bibliographic citations for the materials they use. This information is critical for at least two reasons: they may need to cite the material in a paper or project; or they may need to double-check information or facts from previously used sources. There is a great deal of reference desk-related anecdotal evidence of students asking for a resource, but they only remember the color of the book, what size it was, or which floor it was shelved on. In addition, faculty members sometimes reinforce this behavior when they distribute course syllabi with incomplete or grossly inadequate citations to required course materials. Case in point: as I completed this chapter during a reference desk rotation, a student approached and asked if the library carried a later edition of a textbook. The syllabus entry read: Special Education, 2 ed., Shea and Bauer. A cross-field search of title and author in the UMBC's online catalog revealed one item by the authors with that particular phrase in the title. A follow-up search of the *WorldCat* database revealed, and confirmed, that the complete title was actually: *An Introduction to Special Education: A Social Systems Perspective*, 2 ed., by Thomas M. Shea and Anne M. Bauer, 1997.

Previously used methods for managing information are still popular and reliable today. The use of a note or index card for each bibliographic citation is an extremely reliable method that will usually not fail or be destroyed when your laptop crashes or your disk becomes compromised. However, the loss of a backpack or of a rubber band–bound pack of color-coded index cards could prove to be devastating. Technological advances, including the development of specialized bibliographic management software, make it easy to manage citations for references and bibliographies. In addition, many databases and catalogs facilitate the process by allowing users to save, print, or e-mail search strategies, histories, and results directly from the source itself.

The question of whether to cite sources when quoting or summarizing material is expressly addressed by Standard 5 (see chapter 7), but outcome 2.5.c addresses citation methods and styles in general. Students are often clueless about citation style guides or manuals. It is the responsibility of the faculty within a particular discipline to introduce students to, and instruct them in the use of, style manuals for their particular disciplines. It is also useful if students are instructed as to why they need to be familiar with discipline-specific methods of citation.

Assessment Queries

Current technology makes it easy to organize and manage information electronically. Computing skills such as file management, e-mailing, and word processing are no longer considered specialized. Database and spreadsheet expertise are also frequently considered necessary for sophisticated information management.

Assessing students' ability to manage information using vendor-specific protocols can be achieved without much effort. The following was adapted from the *UMBC Survey* question that asks about students' experience with computers.

> Please select the items that describe your experience with databases and catalogs. Please select all that apply.
>
> a. E-mailed records directly from a library catalog or database
>
> b. Saved records directly from a library catalog or database
>
> c. Printed records directly from a library catalog or database using the database print function (not using the web browser or "print screen")
>
> d. Exported records from a database or catalog using bibliographic management software (e.g., EndNote, ProCite)
>
> e. Copied and pasted records from a catalog or database into a word-processed document
>
> f. Changed the viewing preferences (the way the record or list of results looks) within a catalog or database

A 2001 *Orientation Survey* developed by Caroline M. Stern for her 2002 dissertation endeavored to "assess [the] entry-level digital information literacy of incoming college freshmen." One question from this instrument deals with how students manage information. Although it refers primarily to articles from the Web, this question could be modified to include different types of resources.

If you collected information from web articles for a research paper, how would [you] save the information that you might quote from or paraphrase later? I would . . .

   a. write down or bookmark the URL so I could take notes from the screen later

   b. take notes on the information on the screen and refer to my notes later

   c. "cut and paste" information from the screen to a disc or file

   d. print out a portion of the article to read the information later

   e. print out the whole article to read later and then select the portions I need

In writing assessment queries for outcome 2.5.c., it is important to keep in mind that students are rarely instructed in the differences among citation style methods, nor are they generally aware of which disciplines use which style. The following two queries from the Stern dissertation presume previous knowledge of the American Psychological Association (APA) and the Modern Language Association (MLA) citation styles.

Which of the following includes the most complete list of elements that are typically required for an MLA or APA formatted citation for a *magazine article* from an *online database*?

   a. author, title of article, magazine's title, date of publication, pages, name of the database

   b. author, title of article, magazine's title, magazine publisher, date of publication, pages, name of the database, URL

   c. author, title of article, magazine's title, date of publication, pages, name of the database, URL

   d. author, title of article, magazine's title, date of publication, pages, name of the database, date of access, URL

Which of the following statements is true?

   a. When citing articles you retrieved from an online periodical database, you need to include the name of the database.

   b. Different disciplines, such as psychology or biology, have developed specific citation styles.

   c. The MLA style of citations is used by web search engines.

    d. Answers a and b.

    e. Answers b and c.

The following question addresses managing information. The addition of an "I don't know" option might eliminate guessing and also provide students who don't know the answer with a viable option for responding.

    As you collect sources for your project it is critical to

    a. evaluate each source for accuracy and currency

    b. print the full text out

    c. record all bibliographic information for your Works Cited list

    d. answers a and b.

    e. answers a and c.[22]

Assignments

Very few assignments were identified for this particular performance indicator. Kimberly E. Kelley at the University of Maryland University College advocates having students use software developed to manage bibliographic citations.[23] Students can be required to conduct the research and export records directly from the catalog or database, then automatically generate a bibliography using a specified citation style.

The debate method has been used effectively to instruct college-bound juniors and seniors in the importance of accessing, evaluating, managing, and presenting information for the Black Issues Forum at Colorado State University.[24] Students are assigned roles in case studies depicting critical issues in the African-American community (e.g., images of African-Americans in the media). Students use library resources to research their individual roles (e.g., mother of Honor Roll basketball star shot by white neighbor), and then they participate in a debate or town hall meeting where they are required to cite their sources for credibility. In each of these scenarios, groups of students are required to submit an annotated bibliography, using a particular citation method, that includes all of the resources they used for character development and their presentations.

NOTES

    1. Jeffrey G. Reed, "Information-Seeking Behavior of College Students Using a Library to Do Research: A Pilot Study" (1974), ERIC ED 100 306; Teresa Y. Neely, *Sociological and*

Psychological Aspects of Information Literacy in Higher Education (Lanham, MD: Scarecrow, 2002).

2. Neely, *Sociological and Psychological Aspects*; UMBC Information Literacy Task Force. "UMBC Information Literacy Survey—2003 Executive Summary," Albin O. Kuhn Library & Gallery, University of Maryland, Baltimore County, http://aok.lib.umbc.edu/reference/informationliteracy/ESinfolit2003.pdf.

3. Patricia Daragan and Gwendolyn Stevens, "Developing Lifelong Learners: An Integrative and Developmental Approach to Information Literacy," *Research Strategies* 14, no. 2 (1996): 68–81.

4. Daragan and Stevens, "Developing Lifelong Learners."

5. Sarah Blakeslee, California State University, Chico, "UNIV001C: Introduction to University Life Information Competency Assignment, Choosing the Right Database," http://www.csuchico.edu/lins/IC_grant/sample_assignments/Choosing_Right_Database.doc.

6. Jimmy Ghaphery, Virginia Commonwealth University Libraries, e-mail message to author, March 20, 2003.

7. Neely, *Sociological and Psychological Aspects*, 97, 108.

8. Claudia J. Morner, "A Test of Library Research Skills for Education Doctoral Students" (Ph.D. diss., Boston College, 1993), 152.

9. Kimberly E. Kelley, Information and Library Services, University of Maryland University College, "Information Literacy and Writing Assessment Project: Tutorial for Developing and Evaluating Assignments," http://www.umuc.edu/library/tutorials/information_literacy/sect4.html#sample.

10. Memorial University of Newfoundland, Memorial University Libraries, "Ideas for Library/Information Assignments," http://www.library.mun.ca/qeii/instruction/assignment_ideas.php.

11. Kristin Johnson, Meriam Library, California State University, Chico, "UNIV001C: Introduction to University Life Information Competency Assignment, Using the Library of Congress Subject Headings (LCSH)," http://www.csuchico.edu/lins/IC_grant/sample_assignments/LC_Subject_Headings.doc.

12. Susan E. Beck, New Mexico State University, "LSC 311 Information Literacy, Hands-on #5: Finding Periodicals and Using Print Periodical Indexes. Subject Headings Change Over Time," http://lib.nmsu.edu/instruction/lsc311/beck/assign05.html.

13. Kathy Payne, Stewart Library Information Literacy Team (Chair: Carol Hansen, Instructional Services Librarian), Weber State University, "Using *InfoTrac SearchBank* and Using Yahoo," http://myhome.sunyocc.edu/~weilera/lic/SCLD.html.

14. See Sanford Berman, *Prejudices and Antipathies: A Tract on the LC Subject Heads concerning People* (Metuchen, NJ: Scarecrow, 1971); and Teresa Y. Neely, "Using Subject Terminology and Classification to Provide Effective Service to Diverse Populations," *Colorado Libraries* 21, no. 2 (Summer 1995): 22–26.

15. Central Queensland University Library, "Information Literacy at CQU," http://www.library.cqu.edu.au/informationliteracy/teachresources/resources4standards.html; State University of New York, "Curriculum Relevant to the SCLD Information Literacy Initiative, Concept Mapping," http://library.lib.binghamton.edu/sunyla/curriculum.html.

16. Central Queensland University Library, "Search Strategy Paraphrase," http://www
.library.cqu.edu.au/informationliteracy/teachresources/assess_ideas.htm.

17. Clarence Toomer, "Adult Learner Perceptions of Bibliographic Instructional Services in Five Private Four-Year Liberal Arts Colleges in North Carolina" (Ph.D. diss., North
Carolina State University, 1993).

18. Richard Feinberg, State University of New York Librarians Association, "Curriculum Relevant to the SCLD Information Literacy Initiative, Citation Analysis," http://library
.morrisville.edu/sunyla/lic/SCLD.html.

19. Joan Reitz, Western Connecticut State University Library, "LC Call Number Quiz,"
http://www.wcsu.edu/library/lc_quiz.html.

20. Central Queensland University Library, "What to Do When the Book You Want
Isn't Available," http://www.library.cqu.edu.au/compass/find/book_not_available.htm.

21. Sue Ann Brainard, State University of New York, Geneseo, "Search Scenario," http:
//library.geneseo.edu/~brainard/chapters.htm. See also Sue Ann Brainard, Trudi Jacobson,
and Timothy Gatti, eds., *Teaching Information Literacy Concepts: Activities and Frameworks from the Field* (Pittsburgh: Library Instruction, 2001).

22. Bay Area Community Colleges Assessment Project Team, *Bay Area Community
Colleges Assessment Project: A Two-Part Information Competency Assessment Exam*, http:
//www.topsy.org/ICAP/ICAProject.html. The Bay Area Community Colleges Assessment
Project Team includes Bonnie Gratch-Lindauer, project leader, Pam Baker, Amelie Brown,
Micca Gray, Andy Kivel, Brian Lym, and Topsy Smalley.

23. Kelley, "Tutorial for Developing and Evaluating Assignments."

24. Colorado State University, Office of Admissions, "Black Issues Forum," http://lib
.colostate.edu/research/divandarea/bif/.

Evaluating Information

Teresa Y. Neely with
Simmona Simmons-Hodo

STANDARD 3
The information literate student evaluates information and its sources
critically and incorporates selected information into his or
her knowledge base and value system.

This chapter will discuss the components of evaluation and critical thinking
as outlined in Standard 3. The acquisition and application of this standard's
principles by college-level students are important in both learning and research. The ideal outcome for mastering this standard is that the information-
literate student will have acquired transferable skills that are applicable in
any situation that requires evaluation, critical analysis, and critical thinking.

Standard 3 is one of the most detailed standards, with seven performance
indicators and twenty-five accompanying outcomes. The performance indicators can be characterized as falling into two broad groups: those assessing
students' ability to incorporate selected information into their knowledge
base and value system (3.1, 3.3, 3.6, 3.7), and those assessing students' ability
to evaluate information and its sources critically (3.2, 3.4, 3.5). This chapter
is arranged based on these two groups. For the first group, the key concepts
include the ability to summarize and synthesize main ideas, engage in discourse with others in order to validate understanding, and determine whether
revision of the initial query is necessary. For those in the second group, the

key concepts are evaluation and critical thinking. Together these two groups make up what can be called the most critical skill set in the information literacy framework.[1]

The following sections discuss the key indicators and outcomes under Standard 3, along with examples of assessment questions and sample assignments. Queries and assignments were not identified or developed for every individual indicator and outcome, but the major concepts of the standard are represented. These examples are presented as guides and may be used or adapted to fit your institution's particular needs.

ASSESSING THE ABILITY TO INCORPORATE SELECTED INFORMATION INTO ONE'S KNOWLEDGE BASE AND VALUE SYSTEM

The four performance indicators that make up this first broad group are arguably the most simple at first glance, but they can be the most complex to construct assessment queries and assignments for. In order to successfully summarize main ideas from information sources, the student must be able to identify and understand key concepts from retrieved information, restate those concepts and details accurately by paraphrasing, and identify material that can be quoted. Additionally, the student must be familiar with the definitions for summarizing and paraphrasing and be able to understand and apply these concepts within the context of assignments and other course work. Unfortunately, students get little time to practice critical thinking skills prior to the college-level research environment. They must quickly adapt from regurgitating facts and data to thinking critically, extrapolating, restating, and summarizing. It is imperative that students possess the skills to be able to determine when to paraphrase and when and how much to quote verbatim.

Performance Indicator 3.1. The information literate student summarizes the main ideas to be extracted from the information gathered.

    Outcome 3.1.a. Reads the text and selects main ideas

    Outcome 3.1.b. Restates textual concepts in his/her own words and selects data accurately

> *Outcome 3.1.c.* Identifies verbatim material that can be then
> appropriately quoted

Assessment Queries

Recommended query types for assessing this performance indicator include
those that require the student to demonstrate the ability to successfully complete tasks that represent the skills embodied by the outcomes. The following
three queries were taken from the same instrument and address outcomes
3.1.a, b, and c, respectively.[2]

> In the initial stages of your research, you find this paragraph:

> > Many studies have shown that the more corporal punishment is used
> > in someone's childhood, the greater the probability that the adult
> > will be physically violent. Physical violence to children can become a
> > way of life. Moreover, family violence cuts across all socioeconomic
> > groups.

> The above paragraph provides relevant information for which of the
> following topics?
>
> a. increase in adult violence
>
> b. physical punishment of children
>
> c. relationship between physical punishment of children and
>   adult violence
>
> d. violence and class differences

This query is an excellent example for assessing students' ability to read critically and identify the key focus of a particular passage. The addition of an "I
don't know" option would decrease the likelihood of students' guessing.

> Paraphrasing is the process of
>
> a. summarizing the author's ideas in your own words
>
> b. selecting paragraphs to use in your paper
>
> c. changing a phrase to mean something else
>
> d. none of the above

This query tests a student's knowledge of the concept of paraphrasing. Instead of an "I don't know" option, the query developers included "none of the
above." This option will also prevent the tendency to guess, to some extent.

Read the following extract and select the quotation that would best explain what the NCFL does.

> "Sometimes it takes a creative idea to give power to good intentions. We think the National Center for Family Literacy is a great idea, and that is why Toyota is proud to be one of its major supporters. NCFL is the leader in parent-child learning. It's a powerful way to develop learning skills in young children by helping disadvantaged parents complete their own education and learn important life skills at the same time. Toyota has provided support to more than 150 family literacy programs across America . . ." (From: *U.S. News & World Report*, 10 Dec. 2001: 27)

a. "NCFL is the leader in parent-child learning."

b. "It's a powerful way to develop learning skills in young children by helping disadvantaged parents complete their own education and learn important life skills at the same time."

c. "Sometimes it takes a creative idea to give power to good intentions."

d. "Toyota has provided support to more than 150 family literacy programs across America."

This query provides a realistic information problem that requires a student to read the provided passage critically in order to respond accurately. All of the options are direct quotes from the text, but a student is only asked to select the one that best explains the work of the named organization. This type of query also provides insight into the student's retention and processing skills.

Assignments

The assignments developed for this performance indicator could be very similar to the queries listed above. Students can be required to read a passage, abstract, or article and then prepare a summary that identifies the key concepts represented, along with a copy of the information source itself. Students could also be required to restate, summarize, or paraphrase the passage, abstract, or article as an in-class assignment. Requiring students to complete the assignment during class gives them time to focus specifically on the task at hand with instructor support. Additionally, this assignment contains aspects of outcomes 1.1.e (identifies key concepts and terms that describe the information need) and 2.2.b and c (identifies keywords, synonyms, and related terms and selects controlled vocabulary). In order to paraphrase and restate in their own words, students must be familiar with the topic and with other words and concepts that describe the topic.

Another assignment could require students to prepare a presentation, summarizing the resources they have identified for their research project. Students could identify and justify the selection of key quotations or passages from the information source that would best support their research topic. These assignment examples could also be designed to build upon each other, culminating in a final research paper or annotated bibliography, with scheduled instructor feedback at various intervals throughout the process.

Performance Indicator 3.3. The information literate student synthesizes main ideas to construct new concepts.

> **Outcome 3.3.a.** Recognizes interrelationships among concepts and combines them into potentially useful primary statements with supporting evidence
>
> **Outcome 3.3.b.** Extends initial synthesis, when possible, at a higher level of abstraction to construct new hypotheses that may require additional information
>
> **Outcome 3.3.c.** Utilizes computer and other technologies (e.g., spreadsheets, databases, multimedia, and audio or visual equipment) for studying the interaction of ideas and other phenomena

A review of the survey instruments in the appendix yielded no queries for these particular outcomes. The skill set represented by this performance indicator could be considered higher-order thinking skills. Most college-level students will probably not be expected to master or utilize the skills represented by this performance indicator during their undergraduate education. Most often, these outcomes will be acquired and reinforced by upper-level undergraduates completing senior papers or projects or by graduate students completing master's theses or dissertations.

Performance Indicator 3.6. The information literate student validates understanding and interpretation of the information through discourse with other individuals, subject-area experts, and/or practitioners.

Outcome 3.6.a. Participates in classroom and other discussions

Outcome 3.6.b. Participates in class-sponsored electronic communication forums designed to encourage discourse on the topic (e.g., e-mail, bulletin boards, chat rooms)

Outcome 3.6.c. Seeks expert opinion through a variety of mechanisms (e.g., interviews, e-mail, listservs)

This performance indicator broadly addresses communication skills. In order to participate in course-related discussions, conduct interviews, and use other electronic means of discussion, college-level students need good communication skills, written and otherwise. Specifically, they need to be able to articulate a position on a particular topic and engage in intellectual discourse in order to validate their understanding and interpretation of retrieved information. They also need to be familiar with Internet etiquette, or "netiquette," an established set of rules and conventions for acceptable behavior when communicating electronically.

This performance indicator also contains an aspect of outcome 1.1.a: the information-literate student "confers with instructors and participates in class discussions, peer workgroups, and electronic discussions to identify a research topic, or other information need." Although instructors are not expressly mentioned, it can be inferred that any classroom discussion or class-sponsored communication forum would involve an individual in the instructor role to provide guidance and structure.

Outcome 3.6.c is similar to outcome 2.3.d: the information-literate student "uses surveys, letters, interviews, and other forms of inquiry to retrieve primary information." Students who are proficient with outcome 3.6.c must be aware that the information-seeking process is multifaceted and that information can be obtained from a wide variety of sources, including subject-specific electronic discussion lists populated by professionals in a particular discipline and the experts themselves who publish the information that is indexed in databases and represented in library catalogs.

Assessment Queries

The *UMBC Survey* includes a number of questions designed to assess communication skills. Several queries ask students to self-report their familiarity with a variety of presentation methods. A similar query was developed by the authors to elicit responses on skills represented by this performance indicator:

> In your academic career (high school, community college, college or university), have you ever been given the opportunity to participate in a course that used the following technologies for facilitating communication:
>
> a. instant messaging   f. internal e-mail
> b. bulletin board   g. online journal/notes
> c. threaded discussions   h. real-time chat
> d. discussion forums   i. whiteboard
> e. file exchange   j. other _____

Additional queries can be developed asking students about their experiences participating in course-related discussions, the methods they prefer (online or in person), and their level of comfort with those methods, including the examples provided above.

Assignments

Instructors could easily require students to participate in a number of creative assignments designed to facilitate and encourage course-related discussion. For example, the use of course software such as Blackboard or WebCT provides instructors with the flexibility and capability to create asynchronous and synchronous small-group discussions and allow threaded bulletin board postings on key course topics. Additionally, depending on the discipline and the availability of resources, students could be required to identify, subscribe, and "lurk" on a professional electronic discussion list or discussion group that represents their selected research topic. Students could monitor the discussion list for the entire semester or a specified length of time and then prepare and present (or submit via e-mail or post using course software) a summary of the key current issues discussed by practitioners and researchers who populate the list.

Another assignment could require students to identify a piece of research on their chosen topic, critically analyze that research based on basic evaluation criteria provided by the instructor, and then locate and contact the author and conduct an interview. Each student could then prepare a report that includes a summary of the interview and the list of interview questions, along with key concepts or passages extrapolated from the research that directly supports the student's research thesis.

Each of these assignments could be tailored for a variety of disciplines and audiences. For example, instead of a research article, students could use a dissertation or master's thesis, a short story or poem, a literary text, a book chapter or an essay, or a play or other dramatic narrative. It is important to ensure that when using this assignment, students are cautioned against selecting research or creative works by authors who may be deceased (no opportunity to interview), obscure (too little primary information), or too famous (limited or no opportunity to interview). Ideally, research topics and potential authors would be selected in consultation with the instructor to prevent duplication and determine appropriateness.

Performance Indicator 3.7. The information literate student determines whether the initial query should be revised.

> **Outcome 3.7.a**. Determines if original information need has been satisfied or if additional information is needed
>
> **Outcome 3.7.b**. Reviews search strategy and incorporates additional concepts as necessary
>
> **Outcome 3.7.c**. Reviews information retrieval sources used and expands to include others as needed

This performance indicator is similar in nature to indicator 2.4: the information-literate student refines the search strategy if necessary. In order for students to become proficient with performance indicator 3.7, they must have acquired and reinforced skills from each of the preceding standards (1 and 2) and their accompanying indicators and outcomes; specifically, assessing the original information need and comparing it to the resources they have gathered. Additionally, the ability to broaden or narrow the search strategy is crucial in order to conduct an efficient and effective search for relevant information. Along with the review of the search strategy, it may be necessary to expand the information-seeking process to incorporate other appropriate resources.

Assessment Queries

It has proven to be challenging to develop objective standardized assessment queries for this performance indicator. Because this indicator represents a series of tasks based on a critical analysis of research results, search strategies, and information retrieval sources, student assessment will, for the most part, be based on a self-assessment of their perceptions of the success or failure of their research investigation. Assessment queries for this performance indicator could be similar to those developed for indicator 2.4. Students could be asked to self-report the frequency with which they complete tasks represented by the outcomes for this performance indicator. Some of the following statements were adapted from a query originating from the *Morner Test*. Additional statements were developed by the authors based on outcomes specific to this indicator. An adapted version of the original query also appears in the *Neely Test* and the *UMBC Survey*.

> After you have done your initial research for a paper, how often do you do the following?
>
> a. Review the original research questions/thesis to determine if additional information is needed to satisfy the information need.
>
> b. Review search strategy and search using additional keywords and concepts.
>
> c. Review databases and other information retrieval sources used and identify and search additional ones.

Students' knowledge and mastery of the skills represented by these outcomes could also be assessed by their responses to the questions below. This type of query would not be appropriate for a large-scale assessment, but students could be introduced to these skills as they complete a research paper, presentation, or other project.

> a. What was your original research question/thesis?
>
> b. Which of the information sources gathered provides appropriate support for your original research question/thesis and why?
>
> c. Which of the information sources gathered do not provide appropriate support for your original research question/thesis and why not?

d. What search strategy did you use to identify the information sources gathered?

e. If you need additional sources, what, if any, additional keywords will you use?

f. Which databases and catalogs did you use to identify information and why?

g. If you need additional sources, which, if any, other databases will you use and why?

Assignments

In considering assignments that will help students to become proficient with this performance indicator, an instructor could incorporate the teaching and acquisition of the skills represented by the outcomes with a major project, paper, or presentation. As part of learning the research process, students could be required to respond to a series of questions about the materials they have gathered for their project. Specifically, they could be required to restate their original thesis and indicate which of the identified materials best addresses the information need. This analysis should lead the students to a logical next step of reevaluating the search strategy so that it is more closely aligned with the original thesis, expanding the search and acquiring more information if deemed necessary. A variation on this assignment incorporates peer review. Students could be partnered or divided into small groups. Partners could be required to exchange information sources and conduct an analysis of each other's original research thesis, or students' findings and original thesis analyses could be presented to the group.

ASSESSING THE ABILITY TO EVALUATE INFORMATION AND ITS SOURCES CRITICALLY

This section addresses performance indicators 3.2, 3.4, and 3.5. Together these outcomes represent a critical skill set within the information literacy framework: addressing evaluative criteria, comparing and contrasting new knowledge with prior knowledge, and determining the impact of new knowledge on values. The ability of college-level students to evaluate information and information sources effectively and efficiently has always been a key issue for library and information professionals. The literature reveals that this is a skill with which students are the least confident. Additionally, when students are assessed on this skill, they perform least successfully when compared to other information literacy skills.[3]

Performance Indicator 3.2. The information literate student articulates and applies initial criteria for evaluating both the information and its sources.

> ***Outcome 3.2.a***. Examines and compares information from various sources in order to evaluate reliability, validity, accuracy, authority, timeliness, and point of view or bias
>
> ***Outcome 3.2.b***. Analyzes the structure and logic of supporting arguments or methods
>
> ***Outcome 3.2.c***. Recognizes prejudice, deception, or manipulation
>
> ***Outcome 3.2.d***. Recognizes the cultural, physical, or other context within which the information was created and understands the impact of context on interpreting the information

This particular indicator addresses the heart of the information literacy skill set. Students proficient with the outcomes represented by this indicator know that all sources should be critically analyzed using generally accepted evaluative criteria, regardless of format. Once they have acquired effective evaluation skills, students will be equipped to organize, analyze, and manage all types of information. Library and information professionals have identified a number of core criteria that should be considered when evaluating information and sources of information. The following criteria are adapted from the ACRL's Objectives for Information Literacy Instruction and can be applied to both print and electronic sources.[4]

> *Accuracy*. Is the information verifiable? What is the source of the information presented? Is the data complete?
>
> *Audience*. Who is the intended population for this information? Students? Professionals? Practitioners? Researchers? Educators? Consumers? Customers?
>
> *Author/Authority*. Who is the author or creator of the information? What are their qualifications and background or training? Can

this information be confirmed in biographical sources or other materials?

Bias/Point of View. Does the information present a one-sided view? Does it express opinions rather than facts? Are the information and sources designed to trigger emotions, conjure stereotypes, or promote support for a particular viewpoint or group? Are the conclusions reasonable? Are there references to other sources that confirm or question a point of view?

Currency. Is the information retrieved sufficiently current for the information need?

Publisher/Publication. What is the reputation of the publisher or issuing agency? Are they qualified to publish on this topic?

Scope/Coverage. Does this resource cover the topic adequately? What is the time frame or subject coverage? Is this information for only a specific period? Is it broad in scope or more narrow? Does it provide references to other sources for additional information?

Timeliness. When was the information published?

Validity. Can the information be either confirmed or verified in other sources?

Assessment Queries

Because the ability to evaluate research tools is a critical skill within the information literacy skill set, it is especially important to develop survey queries that assess and measure students' evaluative abilities and test assumptions about their skill levels. The following are examples of queries that can be used to test students' perceptions and abilities related to performance indicator 3.2. These questions cover several important components of information evaluation, including determining the authority of a source, determining a reliable or credible source, screening for bias, and determining relevance. We have also included a separate section on evaluating websites.

The following query was taken from the *FGC Skunk Ape Tutorial* and broadly assesses students' knowledge of and familiarity with evaluative criteria (3.2).

Which criteria should you use to evaluate whether or not a particular source is valuable for your research?

    a. expert author, reliable information, up-to-date, objective

    b. famous author, high Internet search engine ranking, short, up-to-date

    c. famous author, up-to-date, easy to find, large quantity of information

    d. easy to read, Internet availability, visual aids (diagrams, photos), objective

The following question addresses the authority aspect of outcome 3.2.a.

To determine if an author is qualified to write on a specific topic, which of the following would most likely provide trustworthy information about the author's qualifications:

    a. a general encyclopedia

    b. biography index or database

    c. author's web page hosted by the university where he or she is employed

    d. answers a, b, and c

    e. answers b and c [5]

This query focuses on the author's credentials and qualifications as an expert on a particular topic. It requires the student to use critical thinking and problem-solving skills to determine the best place to locate appropriate information on the author.

The following query, taken from the *Neely Test*, investigates the student's perceptions about information found on the Internet and the credibility of the authors or source of that information.

When would you use an article located on the Internet in a research project? Please select all that apply.

    a. article written by an individual with no known subject-related credentials

    b. article written by an individual with a Ph.D.

    c. article written by a well-known scholar in the field

    d. article available from a website ending in .edu and/or connected to a school, college, or university

 e. article published as part of the proceedings of a professional organization on their website

 f. full text of article available

 g. article available from a free website accessible via the World Wide Web

 h. article listed in the syllabus of a professor

 i. not at all

Many of the queries analyzed for this book appeared in numerous survey instruments, and it was difficult to determine which instrument originated the query. The following is one such query that also addresses outcome 3.2.a.

If you were writing a paper on crime in Baltimore and you found a newspaper article with statistics indicating that there was a 10% decline in 2002, which of the following is the next best step?

 a. Verify the accuracy of the figure by comparing with last year's newspaper.

 b. Check the statistics in a government source.

 c. Use the data, being sure to cite the article in your paper.

 d. I don't know.

The following two queries are from the same instrument and are appropriate to other aspects of outcome 3.2.a, including bias, reliability, and timeliness.[6]

You are writing a report on automobile safety and tires. You have found several sources. Which would be the *most trustworthy* because of the likelihood of having objective information?

 a. report from an automobile association

 b. survey from a tire manufacturer

 c. article in an automobile magazine

 d. article in a consumer rights magazine

 e. article in a women's magazine

When evaluating sources of information, the date of the source

 a. is important depending on the topic

 b. should never be more than ten years old

 c. is only critical in medical research

    d. is usually not important if it is a reliable source

Students' personal experiences and inclinations may inhibit their ability to conduct an objective review of materials they intend to use for their research. The following was taken from the *Morner Test* and, in addition to providing insight about the role and reputation of the publisher as a criterion for evaluation, also addresses the bias aspect of outcome 3.2.a.

> When researching a controversial topic in the library, such as prayer in public schools, could you evaluate an article for bias before reading it? Please select only one response.
>
>   a. No. I need to read an article to find bias.
>
>   b. Yes. The abstract usually evaluates the article and notes any bias.
>
>   c. Yes. If the article is reporting research, it should be unbiased.
>
>   d. Yes. The reputation of a journal publisher or author may indicate bias.
>
>   e. I don't know.

This is an important query because often students do not understand that the bibliographic citation and abstract may provide valuable clues about the validity of the content.

In an effort to determine what sources college-level students consider credible and reliable, the *UMBC Survey* included two queries that asked students when (always, sometimes, never) they would consider particular sources credible or reliable for their research. One question included ten items and focused on the print media, and the other question included seventeen items that focused on broadcast and online media. The print media examples included daily newspapers and papers of record (*New York Post, New York Times, Washington Post, Los Angeles Times, Baltimore Sun*), weekly publications (*Entertainment Weekly, Newsweek, Time, People*), themed publications (*Rolling Stone, Vibe, Sports Illustrated*), and monthly fashion magazines (*Ebony, Seventeen,* and *Vogue*). The broadcast media and online news sources are shown below. The intent behind this query was to include programming from as many of the major network, cable, and news outlets as possible. For both queries, the UMBC Task Force made a conscious effort to include nonmainstream publications and media sources (BET), along with those that are more commonly known (CNN).

a. Saturday Night Live's Weekend Update with Tina Fey and Jimmy Fallon

b. The Oprah Winfrey Show

c. The Daily Show with Jon Stewart

d. CNN News/Headline News

e. Cnn.com/Headlinenews.com

f. Wolf Blitzer Reports

g. Crossfire/Meet the Press/The McLaughlin Group

h. Larry King Live

i. NPR news

j. World News Tonight/CBS Evening News/NBC Nightly News/Fox News/Nightline

k. MSNBC.com

l. Rush Limbaugh syndicated radio show/Ken Hamblin syndicated radio show/The Howard Stern show

m. 60 Minutes/Dateline NBC/Primetime

n. Andy Rooney's weekly commentary

o. Black Entertainment Television (BET) News/BET Tonight with Ed Gordon

p. The Today Show/Good Morning America/The Early Show

q. The Tonight Show with Jay Leno/The Late Show with David Letterman

Although these types of queries are clearly self-report in nature, they do provide some insight into which resources and sources of information students consider credible and reliable for research purposes. There are no right or wrong answers for these queries because they solicit students' perceptions of reliability and credibility. This query format could easily be adapted to include subject-based indexes and abstracts, databases, or other types of resources. However, it is important to keep in mind that in order for students to answer honestly, the options must be familiar to them. Providing a list of unfamiliar journal titles, databases, or other resources may yield assessment results that are biased or provide little insight about what students know and believe they know.

Evaluating Websites

The criteria for evaluating websites are primarily the same as those for evaluating print and other resources, but the key elements relevant for this medium are accuracy, authority, currency, coverage, objectivity, and balance in presentation of ideas. Due to the lack of comprehensive oversight, any web page that was accessible yesterday could conceivably change or disappear by tomorrow. Information-literate students need to be aware of the nature of this online medium as an information resource and practice critical thinking and evaluative skills with all information found therein.

The California State University, Dominguez Hills, *Information Competency Assessment Instrument* includes an excellent series of questions on evaluating websites. These queries address outcome 3.2.a and also 3.4.e. Students are provided a link to view a website either as a graphic image or as a live site. They are then asked to respond (yes, no, can't tell) to a series of questions.

> Is there an indication of when the information was created or updated?
>
> Is there information on the author or producer of the website?
>
> Is there information on the author or producer's credentials?
>
> Is there contact information (e.g., e-mail address for the author or producer)?
>
> Does the website cover the topic extensively?
>
> Is the information presented as fact (vs. opinion)?

Additional questions could be developed to address other areas for this performance indicator, including an analysis of the URL to determine the origin, ownership, and domain of the site; questions about the intended audience; links to other sources; and whether the information can be verified in other sources. The *Cal Poly–Pomona Information Competency Assessment* included the following in its list of questions in addition to those given above:

> Does the information appear to be biased?
>
> Is this website offering an authentic service?

In terms of analyzing URLs to determine the credibility of a website for research purposes, Caroline Stern developed the following for her dissertation.

Which of the following sites would offer the best possible school project research information for the following topic:

Rain forest preservation? http://

   a. www.amazon.com

   b. www.savethearth.net/rainforests

   c. www.pbs.org/tal/costa_rica/rainforests

   d. www.geocities.com/~RainForests/

   e. www.nvc.k12.il.us/links/rainforests.htm

These questions assess students' knowledge and understanding of URLs and how to analyze and dissect them. It is a good idea when constructing this type of query to select URLs (real or made up) that are relatively easy for college-level students to decipher. The goal of such queries is to assess students' ability to select and evaluate appropriate resources for use in their course work, in this case a website. Assessing this skill can easily be accomplished with simple URLs such as those presented above.

Additionally, students need to be aware that in the Internet environment anyone can be a publisher and that the content presented on a web page may not always be accurate or appropriate for college-level research. Additionally, students should be familiar with the variety of domain suffixes in order to be able to evaluate websites and their sources. The following query developed by the authors can be used to test students' knowledge of the more commonly used domains.

Match the domain suffix with the type of host that it represents:

.com	U.S. military
.gov	U.S. government
.edu	Commercial or personal sites
.net	Educational sites
.org	Not-for-profit organizations
.mil	Internet infrastructure

Due to the seamless international nature of the Internet, students should also possess a passing knowledge of the makeup of international domains. Most other countries use a two-letter country designation.[7]

An additional query from Stern's dissertation focuses on determining the reliability of a web page when author information is not available.

If you knew nothing about the author of a web page, what would be your best clue as to whether the page was a reliable source to use for school project research?

    a. the URL (http://www . . . .)

    b. date of last update on the page

    c. the quality of the page's graphic design

    d. the links the page has

    e. the advertisements posted on the page

The following query from the *Saint Rose Assessment* addresses the accuracy of web pages (3.2.a). It also touches on 3.4.b (verifying information from other sources) and 3.4.e (questioning the source of the data).

Which of the following is the *best* way to check the accuracy of a web page?

    a. E-mail the author of the web page.

    b. Ask a friend.

    c. Assume that the information is incorrect.

    d. Check the information against information from other sources.

Assignments

Standard 3 encompasses a number of specific skills, including lower-order thinking skills such as selecting main ideas and summarizing, and higher-order thinking skills such as synthesizing, comparing new knowledge with prior knowledge, and considering the impact of information on an individual's value system. Given this broad evaluation spectrum, it may be necessary to teach and reinforce individual aspects of the evaluation process at different stages of students' academic career. Teaching students to critically evaluate resources obtained from all types of sources, including web search engines, may be a challenge. The following assignments are designed to assist in the process.

The librarians at Weber State University developed the "Using *InfoTrac SearchBank* and Using Yahoo" assignment for use with first-year students.[8] The assignment requires students to compare resources found on the Internet with articles found in preselected databases. By comparing the quality of information found in articles from both types of sources, students learn about selecting relevant resources for their topic and also enhance their critical thinking skills.

One excellent assignment for evaluation includes introducing students to fake or hoax websites or fake e-mails. Students can work in small groups to evaluate the websites using instructor-provided criteria or research the validity of a fake e-mail.

One assignment is to provide students with examples of popular urban legends or fake e-mails and require them to conduct research and determine whether or not they are true. Sites such as www.urbanlegends.com can be used to identify additional examples, such as the following ones:

> Tommy Hilfiger's racial comments made on *The Oprah Winfrey Show*
>
> Kentucky Fried Chicken does not use real chicken (study by University of New Hampshire)
>
> The kidney harvesting crime ring
>
> Always check your backseat
>
> AIDS Mary
>
> McDonalds—Are there really hypodermic needles in the play areas?

Another assignment is to provide students with the URLs to fake or deceptive websites and require them to answer a series of questions to determine the sites' accuracy and validity. The questions used can be those presented previously from California State University, Dominguez Hills and Pomona. A few fake websites are the following:

> http://www.martinlutherking.org/: "Martin Luther King, Jr.: A True Historical Examination." This site includes a variety of authentic-looking links such as "Historical Writings" (discussion of works allegedly plagiarized by Dr. King, including his dissertation and sermons); "The Truth about King"; and suggested books (which include titles authored by David Duke).
>
> http://www.whitehouse.org/: This site looks (design, image of the actual White House, and color scheme) and feels like an authentic website for the White House, with links to "News and Events," "The First Lady," and "White House History and

Tours." However, the headlines are a clear giveaway, such as the following one: http://whitehouse.org/news/2004/061904.asp: "Understanding the 9/11 Commission Statements: Vice President Cheney's Select Translations of Delusional Liberal Mumbo-Jumbo into Patriotic Facts."

http://www.dhmo.org/: "The Web site for the Dihydrogen Monoxide Research Division (DMRD), currently located in Newark, Delaware." This is a fake website that uses the correct technical term for "water and its effects as if it were an exotic chemical with dangerous properties."[9]

In both of these assignments, students could be responsible for presenting their findings individually or as part of a group presentation, with an accompanying annotated bibliography that contains citations to materials that confirm or reject the urban legend, website, or e-mail.

Performance Indicator 3.4. The information literate student compares new knowledge with prior knowledge to determine the value added, contradictions, or other unique characteristics of the information.

Outcome 3.4.a. Determines whether information satisfies the research or other information need

Outcome 3.4.b. Uses consciously selected criteria to determine whether the information contradicts or verifies information used from other sources

Outcome 3.4.c. Draws conclusions based upon information gathered

Outcome 3.4.d. Tests theories with discipline-appropriate techniques (e.g., simulators, experiments)

Outcome 3.4.e. Determines probable accuracy by questioning the source of the data, the limitations of the information gathering tools or strategies, and the reasonableness of the conclusions

Outcome 3.4.f. Integrates new information with previous information or knowledge

Outcome 3.4.g. Selects information that provides evidence for the topic

While students may have some prior knowledge of a topic, the investigation for information should introduce new ideas and perspectives that add a new dimension to their present knowledge. Anecdotal evidence indicates that students are skilled at locating and retrieving information on a specific topic, but their ability to integrate new information with prior knowledge may prove to be more challenging.

Assessment Query

The following query directly addresses outcomes 3.4.b and c. It provides students with an information-related dilemma and asks them to draw a conclusion based on the information gathered. This type of query is an excellent example for this performance indicator. Similar queries and assignments based on this particular aspect of the process, such as those used for performance indicator 3.7, could be developed for these outcomes.

> You now own a 1996 Ford Windstar that has given you electrical problems. You need to buy a new car, so you look at the magazine *Consumer Reports*, which says Windstars have fewer than average electrical repair problems. Which of the following is the *most likely conclusion* to make?
>
> a. You should buy another Windstar.
>
> b. *Consumer Reports* is wrong.
>
> c. You have a different model year from the one described in the report.
>
> d. A mechanic damaged your electrical system.[10]

Assignments

In developing assignments that provide an opportunity for students to acquire and reinforce the skills represented by outcomes 3.4.c and f, students could be asked to submit the conclusions they have arrived at based on the information they have gathered. Additionally, students could be asked to provide a comparison, in a narrative or table (visual) format, of the information they discovered and the information they had prior to conducting the research. With regard to performance indicator 3.4.e, students could be asked to conduct an analysis of the information-gathering tools they used, specifically indicating the accuracy of the information retrieved and the scope of the sources used.

Performance Indicator 3.5. The information literate student determines whether the new knowledge has an impact on the individual's value system and takes steps to reconcile differences.

> ***Outcome 3.5.a***. Investigates differing viewpoints encountered in the literature
>
> ***Outcome 3.5.b***. Determines whether to incorporate or reject viewpoints encountered

This performance indicator is similar to 3.4 and involves significant higher-order critical thinking skills. Students proficient with these outcomes understand that the knowledge and values they bring to the research process as individuals play an integral role in whether they reject or incorporate the varying viewpoints they encounter during their research. Additionally, this indicator presumes that students are familiar with and aware of their value systems in terms of information analysis and critical thinking. These two outcomes involve the student bringing some prior knowledge of the research topic to the table, and in doing so prove to be difficult to assess objectively with traditional queries.

NOTES

1. Teresa Y. Neely, *Sociological and Psychological Aspects of Information Literacy in Higher Education* (Lanham, MD: Scarecrow, 2002), 19.

2. Bay Area Community Colleges Assessment Project Team, *Bay Area Community Colleges Assessment Project: A Two-Part Information Competency Assessment Exam*, http://www.topsy.org/ICAP/ICAProject.html. The Bay Area Community Colleges Assessment Project Team includes Bonnie Gratch-Lindauer, project leader, Pam Baker, Amelie Brown, Micca Gray, Andy Kivel, Brian Lym, and Topsy Smalley.

3. Neely, *Sociological and Psychological Aspects*, 25, 98. See also Heather Morrison, "Information Literacy Skills: An Exploratory Focus Group Study of Student Perceptions," *Research Strategies* 15, no. 1 (1997): 7; and Claudia J. Morner, "A Test of Library Research Skills for Education Doctoral Students" (Ph.D. diss., Boston College, 1993).

4. Association of College and Research Libraries, "Objectives for Information Literacy Instruction: A Model Statement for Academic Librarians," http://www.ala.org/ala/acrl/acrlstandards/objectivesinformation.htm.

5. Bay Area Assessment Team, *Bay Area Community Colleges Assessment Project*.

6. Ibid.

7. Register.com, "Domain Name Rules," http://www.register.com.

8. Kathy Payne, Stewart Library Information Literacy Team (Chair: Carol Hansen, Instructional Services Librarian), Weber State University, "Using *InfoTrac SearchBank* and Using Yahoo," http://myhome.sunyocc.edu/~weilera/lic/SCLD.html.

9. WordIQ.com, "DHMO," http://wordiq.com/definition/DHMO.

10. Bay Area Assessment Team, *Bay Area Community Colleges Assessment Project*.

6

Using Information Effectively

Teresa Y. Neely and Katy Sullivan

STANDARD 4
The information literate student, individually or
as a member of a group, uses information effectively
to accomplish a specific purpose.

Standard 4 primarily addresses two areas of information literacy: the ability to organize new information and synthesize it with prior knowledge and the ability to communicate new information in an effective way. The standard is broadly written and thus open to various methods of assessment. Whatever method of assessment is used, it is important to evaluate students' abilities in these areas, along with their perceived abilities. Using methods such as active course learning and collaborative learning exercises can provide insight into the actual abilities of students, while attitudinal assessment can be gathered through the use of carefully developed questions.

Standard 4 has three performance indicators and ten accompanying outcomes. Key concepts for college-level students are the ability to organize information that has been acquired (4.1.a) and the ability to communicate that information effectively and efficiently to accomplish a specific purpose (4.3). In other words, it is important for students to be able to think critically about the information they have acquired in order to organize that information and communicate it in some meaningful way.

Standard 4 represents the stage when a student brings together all of the information he or she has located, accessed, and evaluated, integrates it with his or her prior knowledge, and creates a new research product or performance. It is also the stage where many students get into trouble by cutting, pasting, and plagiarizing.

One notable aspect of Standard 4 is the lack of objectives for its performance indicators and outcomes. When the ACRL Task Force drafted the standards, it noted that some performance indicators refer to components of learning and instruction that are not typically addressed by librarians. "Objectives were written only for Performance Indicators in the Competency Standards that could be addressed by the librarian or by the librarian and course instructor collaboratively."[1] Standard 4 is one such standard, as are some of the performance indicators in standards 1, 2, 3, and 5. However, the task force members did note that in situations such as these, "librarians could, of course, help course instructors develop objectives in these areas."[2]

One of the challenges in creating tools to assess students for this standard is that it is difficult to measure objectively. Because this standard pertains to how a student approaches a research assignment, most of the research data that has been published relies on student self-assessment. Perhaps for this reason, our review of more than seventy information literacy survey instruments revealed very few survey questions developed for the performance indicators and outcomes of Standard 4.

When writing questions to assess the performance indicators for this standard and developing assignments to assist students in the mastery of the accompanying outcomes, ask yourself the following questions: Can this particular skill be measured objectively? If not, will self-reported/self-assessment data be sufficient for my assessment purposes? For many of the standards, self-assessment data may not be sufficient or reliable. However, if librarians and faculty want to have an idea of, say, what types of presentations and projects students have had to produce (4.3), and what they say they can produce (if given an opportunity), self-assessment data can provide some useful information. It is important to determine ahead of time what type of student response will be acceptable and useful for assessment purposes. This will also assist in the reliability of the questions, ensuring that you are asking the right questions to get the data you need.

ASSESSING THE ABILITY TO ORGANIZE, PLAN, AND CREATE INFORMATION

Performance Indicator 4.1. The information literate student applies new and prior information to the planning and creation of a particular product or performance.

> ***Outcome 4.1.a.*** Organizes the content in a manner that supports the purposes and format of the product or performance (e.g., outlines, drafts, storyboards)
>
> ***Outcome 4.1.b.*** Articulates knowledge and skills transferred from prior experiences to planning and creating the product or performance

Assessment Queries

The library literature contains numerous studies that report on the information-seeking abilities of college students.[3] However, published research on the *demonstration* of students' skills is more elusive. This is due, in part, to the self-report nature of information-seeking behavior research. Very few assessment queries were identified that address this performance indicator.

Outcome 4.1.a focuses on students' ability to organize information in a way that supports the proposed end product (a research paper, oral presentation, etc.). When writing assessment questions for these outcomes, the UMBC Task Force wanted to find out whether students logically follow the steps of the research process, specifically those steps that represent organizing information. One question asked students to indicate how often (very frequently, frequently, occasionally, infrequently, never) they have completed steps in the research process. Although this question is self-report in nature, it does provide some indication of what students say they do, as well as what they say they don't do.

> After you have done your initial research for a paper, how often do you do the following?
>
> a. Understand all of the information.
>
> b. Discuss findings with friends and colleagues.
>
> c. Make an outline.

    d. Review the original research questions to determine if additional information is needed.

    e. Discard irrelevant or useless information.

    f. Revise outline based on research findings.

    g. Look at materials under each outline heading and synthesize major points and concepts.

The key responses to this query are c, f, and g. It is generally known that an outline is crucial in organizing research findings. In fact, this step should be initiated early on, at the point of "defining and articulating an information need" (1.1). The development of a topical outline based on findings helps to organize the material in a logical way. Additionally, by "understanding all of the information" (response a) and participating in a "discussion of findings" (response b), the student is engaging in outcome 4.1.b and is effectively "articulating knowledge and skills transferred from prior experiences." Discussing findings with friends and colleagues allows students to recall and voice (articulate) relevant knowledge and thoughts from previous experiences.

> ***Outcome 4.1.c***. Integrates the new and prior information, including quotations and paraphrasings, in a manner that supports the purposes of the product or performance

In today's information environment, college-level students are expected to possess the ability to integrate knowledge and skills from prior experiences into their academic work such as the completion of course assignments and degree requirements. In addition, they are expected to blend prior knowledge with newly acquired information to create a new product or performance.

    Plagiarism and the misuse or unethical use of information become more apparent at this stage in the research process. One reason for this is that many teaching faculty fail to update or revise assignments, or they assign large classes the same assignment year after year. The prevalence of full-text databases and the reported frequent use of nonproprietary Internet resources by students at all levels also contributes to the temptation to cut and paste information to complete assignments.

    One question taken from the *UMBC Survey* was adapted from the *Neely Test*, in part, to address students' critical thinking skills and practices in the development of new research products. More specifically, it deals with the general manner in which students combine their previous knowledge and opinions on a topic with the opinions of others derived from their library research findings.

> When writing up information found for a research project or for a research presentation, which of the following do you usually do? Please select all that apply.
>
> a. Present what you believe the author(s) said.
> b. Present what you thought your instructor wanted to hear.
> c. Present the opinions of the author(s) verbatim.
> d. Present your own opinions only.
> e. Present a combination of reflection and opinions (yours and author[s]').
> f. Present a combination of reflection and opinions (yours and author[s]') and previously read material.
> g. Present the opinions of the author(s) verbatim in quotation marks.
> h. None of the above.

On a basic level, this question addresses the propensity to plagiarize by not acknowledging the source of ideas and thoughts other than your own. Technically, there is no correct response to this item. The purpose of the question is to find out what students do when presenting or writing information. Ideally, we hope they will select items f and g. (For a more in-depth discussion and examples on plagiarism and the ethics of information, see chapter 7.)

Assignments

The following assignments will introduce students to Standard 4 and assist in their acquisition and mastery of the skills represented by outcomes 4.1.a–c.

Librarians at the Memorial University of Newfoundland Libraries developed a "Read the References" assignment in which students are required to select a research article and read the articles cited by it.[4] Students are instructed to

> explain how each article is related to the original article

consider under what circumstances it is appropriate to cite other papers

determine what different purposes the citations serve

The outcome of this assignment is that the student learns when it is appropriate to recognize the contributions of other authors in the development of new work. The student also learns how numerous sources are organized, synthesized, and summarized and how new and prior information are integrated, including the use of quotations and paraphrasings. This assignment would also be appropriate for performance indicator 5.3 (acknowledging the use of information sources in the communicating of the product or performance).

Andy Geoghegan at Longview Community College (Missouri) has created a critical thinking assignment called "Jumping to Conclusions" that provides students with research conclusions that assess their abilities to determine a good argument from a bad one.[5] Students are required to determine if the argument used is erroneous or is justified by facts. By analyzing these research situations, students build their "information processing skills," as well as their skills in integrating new and prior information that supports the purposes of the product, which, in this case, is determining which argument is appropriate for their research. This assignment would also be appropriate for Standard 3 (evaluating information). The questions could be tailored for a particular course or academic discipline. Some of the questions posed by the creators are the following:

An investigator gave a personality test to a large number of crack cocaine addicts. The addicts' scores on the trait of "emotionality" were significantly lower than the scores on that trait obtained from the general population. This caused the investigator to believe that highly unemotional people are more susceptible to crack cocaine addiction.

A clinic sponsoring a Stop Smoking treatment program surveyed all the people who completed the program during its first year. The survey revealed that 74% of the respondents were still not smoking three months after completing the program. In its next advertising campaign, the clinic claimed a 75% success rate for those who enrolled in its program.

A guest expert on a TV talk show claims that the divorce rate for interracial marriages is five times higher than the divorce rate for same-race marriage partners and urges the viewers to avoid marrying someone of a different race.

A large sample of people of all ages was given an IQ test. It was noted that people over fifty generally had lower IQ scores, and it was concluded that intelligence declines with age.

Another assignment from Longview Community College is called "Facts, Opinions, and Reasoned Judgments."[6] In this assignment, students are given definitions for the terms *fact*, *opinion*, and *reasoned judgment*. Afterward they are provided with a list of questions to consider when evaluating information in any format. Detailed flowcharts conceptualizing the step-by-step process are also included. Figure 6-1 shows the questions developed to distinguish fact from opinion. In this assignment, students enhance critical thinking skills as well as practice synthesizing and integrating information.

> ***Outcome 4.1.d***. Manipulates digital text, images, and data, as
> needed, transferring them from their original locations and
> formats to a new context

Assessment Queries

Technological advances continue to outpace actual skills acquisition even at the college level. Colleges and universities are aware of the gap between needed skill levels and the actual skill levels of incoming freshmen, as well as continuing students, and the impact of this on their success in higher education. In addition to this, there is a real need to graduate students who are prepared with adequate technological skills to compete in a global marketplace.

Assessment questions for this outcome can be approached in a number of ways. You can ask students what skills they possess, you can ask them to self-assess on a set of skills (comfortable, very comfortable, etc.), or you can ask them to respond to questions that require them to demonstrate expertise or knowledge of a skill. The following list of skills (after fig. 6-1) is not meant to be comprehensive but was compiled to provide baseline information on the breadth and variety of technological skills that students are expected to know and have mastered by the time they reach college. Questions for aspects of technological competencies should, ideally, be developed based on the needs and requirements for students at your institution.

Determining Opinions	Determining Facts
Does the author use words that interpret or label, such as: pretty, ugly, safe, dangerous, evil, attractive, well-dressed, good, and so on?	Can the fact be verified by direct observation?
Are there words that clue you to statements of opinion, such as: probably, perhaps, usually, often, sometimes, on occasion, I believe, I think, in my opinion, I feel, I suggest?	Can the facts be trusted? How did the author come to the facts?
Can you identify differing opinions and their effect on the author's views?	Does the author have the skill and experience to make such a statement?
Does the truth of the premise depend on us accepting a certain definition of key words or concepts? Has the author defined the conditions for using the concepts?	Are the facts presented in an objective manner? (any bias evident or suspected?)
	Does the author make clear the sources of statements from authorities? Are these authorities reliable?
	Can the study that generates the facts be duplicated?
	Are the facts relevant to the point being made?
	Have unfavorable or negative points been left out? (Are there counter-studies?)
	Do the facts prove the claim being made or do they merely suggest that the claim is reasonable?

FIGURE 6-1
Opinions vs. Facts

E-mail, preferably web-based, in order to e-mail web pages, citations, library catalog records, and full-text (text, HTML, PDF) journal articles by either using the database e-mail program or by attaching documents (text, images, etc.) to an e-mail message

Online file-management capabilities such as creating, opening, and closing documents (word processing, plain or rich-text, image, audio, video) and folders; and creating and saving/burning files and documents to disks (hard drive, floppy, zip, CD)

Electronic file and folder organization skills for file management and retrieval in a Windows-based environment

Word-processing skills, including the ability to navigate using the tab, home, end, and arrow keys; to format using bold, italicize, underline; to change fonts (size and style); insert items (page numbers, end/footnotes, files, images); copy, cut, and paste text; add, edit, and delete text; use page setup (set and change page margins, paper size, orientation, and layout); use spell check; and print a document[7]

In an attempt to assess the technological skills of students enrolled in her Science 100 course, Karin Readel at the University of Maryland, Baltimore County, developed an instrument that contained the following questions:

What word-processing program do you most commonly use (name and version)?

Do you know how to convert a document to Rich Text Format (an .rtf file)?

Do you know how to scan a document (or disk) for viruses?

Do you know how to FTP a file?

Another approach would be to require written, short-answer responses, such as in the first query about word-processing programs. The latter three questions simply require students to respond using "yes" or "no." These types of questions work best when there are accompanying questions that require the students to demonstrate their knowledge of a particular concept or skill. Librarians at Colorado State University developed core computer competencies for staff and an accompanying *CSU Libraries Minimum Competency Survey* (*CSU Minimum Competency Survey*). Although the questions they developed based on the training proved to be too simplistic, their approach to query development is ideal for this outcome.

Which of these three buttons would you use to maximize a window?

I don't know _____

This query provides a visual representation of the act of maximizing a window. This approach could also be used to illustrate and assess aspects of e-mailing, word processing, and other Windows-based software.

How do you get to Task Manager [to allow you to shut down programs that are not responding]? Select all that apply.

a. ____ press Control, Alt, Delete simultaneously

b. ____ right click on the Task Bar and choose Task Manager

c. ____ right click on the Desktop and choose Properties

d. ____ turn off/reset the computer

e. ____ I don't know

Which of the following would *not* work to move a file or folder? Select all that apply.

a. ____ highlight the file/folder and use the arrow key to move it over

b. ____ cut and paste

c. ____ drag and drop

d. ____ copy and paste

e. ____ I don't know

Match the file extension to the type of document it represents:

a. .txt   ____ MS Excel

b. .doc   ____ Text

c. .htm, .html   ____ MS Word

d. .jpg   ____ Acrobat Reader

e. .mdb   ____ MS PowerPoint

f. .xls   ____ MS Access

g. .ppt   ____ Graphic

h. .pdf   ____ Web Page

The questions on Task Manager and on moving files and folders require a student to know how to perform specific tasks, and the question on file extensions requires a student to demonstrate his or her knowledge of software and file formats by matching a particular extension to its software originator. These types of questions are ideal for ascertaining exactly what students know and know how to do, specifically in terms of outcome 4.1.d.

The following question from the *UMBC Survey* was adapted from the *Neely Test* and asks students to describe their interaction with computers.

> Please select the items that describe your experience with computers. Please select all that apply.
>
> I use computers for:
>
> a. e-mail/chat rooms/IM
> b. word processing/spreadsheets
> c. searching databases
> d. Internet/World Wide Web
> e. games/entertainment
> f. work-related/telecommuting
> g. other: _____

This question assumes that students use computers; however, it does not attempt to investigate their competency level. It was written simply to determine what students use computers for.

A review of the information literacy instruments identified several questions from the *UW Information Literacy* questionnaire that were also appropriate for this performance indicator.

> From the following list, mark all the situations in which you have used the Internet:
>
> ___ to read a newsgroup
> ___ to transfer files
> ___ to get software
> ___ to write and send correspondence
> ___ to participate in online discussion groups
> ___ to browse the Web
> ___ to create a web page

This query asks respondents to indicate under which circumstances they have used the Internet. Responses to this query provide insight into whether or not students have transferred files, downloaded and installed software, and wrote and sent correspondence electronically.

> From the following list, mark all the situations in which you have used electronic mail:
>
> ___ to ask a teacher/instructor a question
>
> ___ to schedule a meeting for a group project
>
> ___ to turn in assignments
>
> ___ to discuss with classmates an issue raised in one of your classes
>
> ___ general chat
>
> ___ to keep in contact with friends and family
>
> ___ other (please specify): _____

Responses to this query provide insight into students' skill level in using e-mail. Asking students if they use e-mail elicits a yes or no response with little more insight; however, this query requires responses to specific instances of e-mail use. For example, in order to turn in assignments, students should be familiar with the attachment option in e-mail and with electronic file and directory organization. In order to schedule a meeting for a group project, they need to be able to identify e-mail addresses, communicate effectively (using the reply or reply all function), and organize multiple e-mails.

The use of citation management software such as ProCite and EndNote is fast becoming popular. This software, which was developed to facilitate the management of citations for bibliographies and notes, requires additional technological skills and could be considered a higher-order skill for this standard. However, in terms of technological competency, in order to make the best use of these bibliographic management tools, students need more than basic computer skills.

Assignments

There were no specific assignments identified for this particular outcome, but students can be instructed to perform certain tasks that demonstrate their knowledge and mastery of the technological skills needed to manipulate digital text, images, and data. For example, students could demonstrate their ability to attach a document (full-text article in the HTML or PDF file formats), image, or other file to an e-mail message and send it; retrieve a document, image, or file attached to an e-mail message; or copy and paste an image or file from one location to another. The appropriate use of word-processing software packages, PowerPoint, and other presentation software also demonstrates expertise with this outcome.

ASSESSING THE ABILITY TO REVISE THE DEVELOPMENT PROCESS FOR THE RESEARCH PRODUCT

Performance Indicator 4.2. The information literate student revises the development process for the product or performance.

> ***Outcome 4.2.a.*** Maintains a journal or log of activities related to the information seeking, evaluating, and communicating process
>
> ***Outcome 4.2.b.*** Reflects on past successes, failures, and alternative strategies

The outcomes accompanying this performance indicator illustrate the process that Carol C. Kuhlthau describes in her extensive research on high school students.[8] This performance indicator could be considered a lower-level skill, not because it is not important for college-level students but because maintaining logs of information-seeking activities is not an activity that is included or emphasized in most college-level instruction and information literacy programs, as evidenced in the published literature.

The UMBC Task Force did not write assessment questions for this performance indicator, and none of the information literacy instruments reviewed contained specific questions for this indicator or its two outcomes.

Assignments

There are a number of assignments that advocate the use of journaling for some aspects of most of the standards. The most common require the student to maintain a log of his or her progress in writing a research paper, including the changing focus of the paper relative to topic development and the search for information. This type of assignment requires students to think critically about the research process and organizing and presenting information. Jack Bales at the University of Mary Washington (Virginia) has developed a resource for a History 299 course that encourages students to maintain a research log to "keep track of [their] resources and search procedures."[9] The professor tells students, "Every time you find something that might be useful, whether it is from a book, an index, or an idea from a person, make a note of it in your research log, which helps you to plot a logical pattern through the library as you look for information on your topic." He reviews the logs periodically throughout the semester, and students receive a numerical grade that counts toward their final grade for the course. This type of assignment also allows students to self-evaluate their progress and growth over time.

ASSESSING THE ABILITY
TO COMMUNICATE INFORMATION

Performance Indicator 4.3. The information literate student communicates the product or performance effectively to others.

> *Outcome 4.3.a*. Chooses a communication medium and format that best supports the purposes of the product or performance and the intended audience
>
> *Outcome 4.3.b*. Uses a range of information technology applications in creating the product or performance
>
> *Outcome 4.3.c*. Incorporates principles of design and communication
>
> *Outcome 4.3.d*. Communicates clearly and with a style that supports the purposes of the intended audience

Assessment Queries

In order for students to engage an audience and effectively communicate the information they have gathered and organized, they need to appeal to all styles of learners. A student who is familiar with a variety of presentation skills and methods is better prepared to accomplish this. For the most part, the communication medium or format is determined by the assignment and the instructor who assigns it. Depending upon their academic major, student status (undergraduate, graduate), and the specific assignment, students have a variety of ways to present information. The *UMBC Survey* contains two questions for outcomes 4.3.a–b, to find out what methods of communication and presentation students have been exposed to and, if given the opportunity, which methods they would feel comfortable using.

> In your academic career (high school, community college, college, or university,), have you ever been given the opportunity to present your research using the following methods/formats? Please select all that apply.
>
> a. written research paper
> b. visual project
> c. presentation using PowerPoint or other presentation software
> d. presentation using nontechnical methods (flip charts, overhead transparencies, etc.)
> e. web pages/site
> f. dramatic performance (singing/dancing/recitation/musical interpretation)
> g. CD
> h. DVD
> i. VHS
> j. other
> k. none of the above

This question was revised so that students were asked to indicate which of the methods (listed above) they would feel comfortable using if given the option.

Successful presentations are also dependent on the presenter's mastery of and comfort with the technology he or she uses. The greater exposure a student has to presentation technologies and methods, the more comfortable he or she will be during the presentation. Today, as our communications media become more and more dependent on technology, students are expected to be able to share and present information in a variety of ways in order to be prepared for academic and lifelong success.

Additional questions for this performance indicator could be grouped to elicit a range of responses, such as the ones developed by Karin Readel at the UMBC:

7. Do you have any experience constructing web pages?

8. If yes, please rank your abilities constructing web pages on a scale of 1 to 10:

   1   2   3   4   5   6   7   8   9   10
   BEGINNER   INTERMEDIATE   ADVANCED

9. If you answered yes to question 7, what software do you use to create web pages?

This type of approach to assessment groups questions on a particular topic together, and each one builds upon the other. If a student responds affirmatively to question 7, yet cannot identify a software in 9, then the student most likely has misrepresented his or her capabilities in 7. This type of query can also be used to assess students' mastery of word-processing skills and other presentation methods as well.

Assignments

The most common assignments for college-level students are research papers and/or accompanying presentations. The following assignments have been identified to introduce students to and reinforce the skills represented by this performance indicator and its outcomes.

Beth L. Mark, instruction coordinator at the Messiah College Library (Pennsylvania), collaborated on an assignment with faculty members from the Health Education and Sports Medicine Department.[10] Students are required to create a newsletter on a particular topic, for example, training/sports medicine/ health issues. The students are encouraged to gear their newsletter toward a fictitious yet realistic audience, such as coaches, rehabilitation faculty, and so on. In this way, they are learning that information can be organized and communicated to different audiences in a variety of ways. They also learn that the final product or presentation is likely to be more effective when the information is presented in an appropriate format. This assignment demonstrates proficiency with outcome 4.3.a.

In addition to creating a newsletter, students can be instructed to develop a web page, a website, or a special subject journal or magazine issue to communicate information to an audience that might include their course colleagues, departmental faculty, conference attendees, or the news media. Students could also prepare a presentation for a potential employer that is appropriate for their major or profession. For example, students could work as a team to prepare a presentation for a marketing course geared toward landing an account for an advertising firm.

Librarians at the University of Puget Sound (Washington) advocate an assignment called "Create an Anthology."[11] Students are required to create an "annotated book of readings." The guidelines for this assignment can include limitations on the type of items annotated; for example, only scholarly sources produced "within the last ten years," or broader limits that include "chapters or excerpts from monographs and significant older materials." Other guidelines include:

> introduction written by students
>
> each included item annotated (including a description and justification for inclusion)
>
> bibliography of items considered for inclusion
>
> appendix of copies of items selected

This assignment is in fact appropriate for several of the standards, in that students learn and use the skills of locating articles, evaluating and selecting appropriate articles for inclusion, and—in the case of outcomes 4.3.a through d— honing their writing skills and communicating the product (i.e., the anthology).

Each of these assignments requires students to select a communication medium for a particular audience, use a range of technology, and communicate a well-designed product. These assignments not only represent Standard 4 but address technological competence as well.

Other methods of communicating information could be less technical, such as a poster presentation, which would still require a student to conduct research on a particular topic and organize and synthesize resources for presentation purposes. For this performance indicator of the standard, students should be allowed the flexibility and creativity to present information using a variety of formats.

NOTES

1. Association of College and Research Libraries, "Objectives for Information Literacy Instruction: A Model Statement for Academic Librarians," http://www.ala.org/ala/acrl/acrlstandards/objectivesinformation.htm.

2. Ibid.

3. See Joseph Atkinson and Miguel Figueroa, "Information Seeking Behavior of Business Students: A Research Study," *Reference Librarian* 58 (1997): 59–73; Bryn Geffert and Beth Christensen, "Things They Carry: Attitudes toward, Opinions about, and Knowledge of Libraries and Research among Incoming College Students," *Reference and User Services Quarterly* 37, no. 3 (1998): 279–89; and Vivian Cothey, "A Longitudinal Study of World Wide Web Users' Information-Searching Behavior," *Journal of American Society for Information Science and Technology* 53, no. 2 (1992): 67–78.

4. Memorial University of Newfoundland, Memorial University Libraries, "Ideas for Library/Information Assignments," http://www.library.mun.ca/qeii/instruction/assignment_ideas.php.

5. Andy Geoghegan, Longview Community College, "Critical Thinking across the Curriculum Project: Psychology Exercises, Jumping to Conclusions," http://www.kcmetro.cc.mo.us/longview/ctac/psychexer1.htm.

6. Patty Illing and Michael Connelly, Longview Community College, "Critical Thinking across the Curriculum Project: Facts, Opinions, and Reasoned Judgments," http://www .kcmetro.cc.mo.us/longview/ctac/opinion.htm.

7. Michael Romary and Reference Department, Albin O. Kuhn Library & Gallery, University of Maryland, Baltimore County, "Minimum Technological Competencies for Incoming Students at UMBC 2002" (working paper).

8. Carol C. Kuhlthau, "Developing a Model of the Library Search Process: Cognitive and Affective Aspects," *Reference Quarterly* 28 (1988): 232–42; Carol C. Kuhlthau, "Information Search Process: A Summary of Research and Implications for School Library Media Programs," *School Library Media Quarterly* 18 (1989): 19–25; Carol C. Kuhlthau, "Inside the Search Process: Information Seeking from the User's Perspective," *Journal of the American Society for Information Science* 42 (1991): 361–71.

9. Jack Bales, University of Mary Washington, "History 299 Materials: The Library and the Research Log," http://www.mwc.edu/hisa/resources/writing/299/researchlog_299.htm.

10. Beth L. Mark, Messiah College Library, "Creating Newsletters," http://library.morrisville.edu/sunyla/lic/SCLD.html.

11. Lori Ricigliano, University of Puget Sound, "Ideas for Library Related Assignments," http://library.ups.edu/instruct/assign.htm.

7

Information, Social Context, and Ethical and Legal Issues

Olga François

STANDARD 5
The information literate student understands many of the economic,
legal, and social issues surrounding the use of information
and accesses and uses information ethically and legally.

Major advances in information technology have led to great increases in the volume and diversity of available and publicly accessed information sources in all media. This change has placed increased demands on college-level students' understanding of how information is produced, stored, and accessed. Standard 5 is concerned with students' understanding of the economic, legal, and social issues surrounding the use of information and with their access and use of information in ethical and legal ways. The standard encompasses broadly cast issues of the information environment, contextual ideas of knowledge construction, and pragmatic questions of law and policy.

Standard 5 has three performance indicators and thirteen accompanying outcomes. The standard is complex, somewhat philosophical, and above all requires students to think critically about information issues. Student outcomes relating to these issues can be summarized as the ability to understand and apply local and national information policies (such as acceptable-use policies and copyright) in multiple contexts; to demonstrate an understanding of the conventions and implications of scholarly, mass market, and not-for-profit publishing; to interact ethically with information and its technologies; and to recognize the social and political implications inherent in information production and systems.

A body of work is just beginning to emerge, with very few completed studies, which expands our understanding of how to teach Standard 5 beyond proper citation and basic definitions of copyright and fair use.[1] It may be tempting to focus teaching and assessment processes on these easily quantifiable objectives within the standard and neglect the social structure literacy questions that Shapiro and Hughes discuss.[2] However, as illustrated in this chapter, survey queries can be constructed to assist in informing curriculum design and the development of student skills in this vital area. Students cannot make ethical decisions about information use or develop informed research strategies if they do not recognize the social and political implications of information systems. The assignment examples and assessment queries offered are not meant to be prescriptive; rather, they illustrate a variety of ways to adapt the standard to serve both institutional and student assessment needs. Please note that outcome 5.2.f will be discussed in the final section with performance indicator 5.3.

ASSESSING THE UNDERSTANDING OF KNOWLEDGE PRODUCTION AND INFORMATION ACCESS

Performance Indicator 5.1. The information literate student understands many of the ethical, legal, and socioeconomic issues surrounding information and information technology.

> ***Outcome 5.1.a.*** Identifies and discusses issues related to privacy and security in both the print and electronic environments
>
> ***Outcome 5.1.b.*** Identifies and discusses issues related to free versus fee-based access to information
>
> ***Outcome 5.1.c.*** Identifies and discusses issues related to censorship and freedom of speech
>
> ***Outcome 5.1.d.*** Demonstrates an understanding of intellectual property, copyright, and fair use of copyrighted material

Performance indicator 5.1 asks that students understand the intricate and diverse contexts in which they are working and researching. Although as educators we may recognize that the work we do has political and social ramifications, these issues are seldom directly addressed in the theoretical literature of information literacy and library instruction.[3] This performance indicator requires a complex and content-based approach in the curriculum, in contrast with more tool- or skill-based performance indicators. It challenges librarians to teach the larger context of information issues within information literacy curricula and programs.

Assessment Queries

To raise students' understanding of the complexity of the issues surrounding Standard 5, it is best to apply methods of instruction and assessment on the course and assignment level that give the instructor an opportunity to gain an understanding of what students know in order to make changes in teaching and learning opportunities during the course itself. This type of assessment is known as formative assessment, and its use gives students the opportunity to see the gap between their current knowledge and the stated goal.[4] It is difficult to assess the development of advanced skills in a survey, and this is especially true for performance indicator 5.1.

Otterbein College's *Survey of College Students regarding Copyright Law Information* provides several excellent questions to assess students' understanding of the concept of copyright and their ability to identify issues related to free and fee-based information. The following queries rely on self-perception and reporting:

How often do you copy multiple chapters of books?

How often do you download MP3 files from peer-to-peer file-sharing networks (e.g., Kazaa)?

How often do you share licensed computer software with others?

In your opinion, is it okay to make a compilation CD for a friend from CDs you purchased?

The following are true-or-false queries to directly test students' knowledge:

Copyright law protects both published and unpublished works.

Architectural works are not protected by copyright laws.

Copyright law protects ideas and facts.

Legal action for infringement can only be taken once the work is registered with the U.S. Copyright Office.

Copyright laws do not protect slogans or logos.

It is legal for a professor to tape a program off of television and show it to the class.

The queries above could be supplemented with the following ones to more completely address the performance indicator:

In your opinion, is it okay to bypass the security system on a DVD to get it to run on a player purchased in another country?

True or False—The First Amendment guarantees freedom of speech for all U.S. citizens.

True or False—Preventing a student from stating their personal opinion in an essay is censorship.

There is a challenge in surveying students' knowledge and application of laws that are themselves open to interpretation, like the copyright law. The *UMBC Survey* asks the following questions, allowing the student to respond either "yes," "no," or "don't know" for each item listed.

Copyright is a form of protection provided by the laws of the United States to the authors of "original works of authorship," including literary, dramatic, musical, artistic, and certain other intellectual works. This protection is available for both published and unpublished works. If you were creating your own website, which of the following could you legally use on your web page without permission?

   a. Pictures of Britney Spears from the Internet

   b. The theme song from *Titanic* by Celine Dion

   c. Letters that you found at the National Archives written by Martha to her husband, President George Washington

   d. President George W. Bush's Inaugural Speech

   e. Pictures of Anna Kournikova scanned in from *Sports Illustrated* magazine

   f. Text you scanned in of *Harry Potter and the Prisoner of Azkaban*

   g. Text of the Homeland Security Act introduced in Congress

   h. Text of an article from *Newsweek* that you scanned in criticizing the Homeland Security Act

The phrase "use without permission" indicates either that an item does not meet the "originality" requirement for issuing exclusive copyrights, that it is in the public domain (copyright terms having expired or its author having deemed it a public domain document and granted open access), or that its use fits within the "fair use" provisions of the U.S. Copyright Act. The query above would evaluate a student's knowledge of the exemption for U.S. government works (17 U.S.C. §105) absolutely (items d and g) and for copyright term expiration (item c). The use of any of the others would only be permissible if that use was in the context of a student's academic work, in which case the "fair use" provision might apply. For an advanced student, this query could be enhanced with an "it depends" answer choice. Additional questions can also be asked of the scenario presented in order to fully assess outcomes 5.1.d and 5.2.e: How much of the items listed will be used or scanned? Will the reproduction of it be on the intranet or Internet? The query could be enhanced by articulating the purpose of the website: is it on the World Wide Web for personal use and mass public display?

   Another query from the *UMBC Survey* focuses specifically on fair use (5.1.d):

> One of the limitations to *copyright* law is the doctrine of *fair use.* This provision allows for the "fair" reproduction of a particular work for purposes such as criticism, comment, news reporting, teaching, scholarship, and research. If you were preparing an assignment for class, which of the following could you legally do?
>
>   a. For your research paper on Tupac Shakur, directly quote, without citing a source, a paragraph from an article titled "The Miseducation of Hip-Hop," published in the journal *Black Issues in Higher Education.*
>
>   b. Use a video clip from the *Rosie O'Donnell Show* as part of a class presentation on talk shows.
>
>   c. Use an audio clip of "I Want to Hold Your Hand" by the Beatles as part of a class presentation on relationships.

    d. Use music from the Rolling Stones or Sean "P. Diddy" Combs as background music during a presentation.

    e. Report on and summarize an article on depression and longevity from the *American Journal of Geriatric Psychiatry* in a speech for your psychology class.

    f. Make a copy of a book chapter placed on reserve in the library by your professor and take it home to read.

Formative assessment might assess a student's course assignments and class or workshop discussions for the following high-level skills:

> Can the student articulate the changes in the publication "chain" from published scientific studies to popular reporting in the mass media?

> Can the student describe various pricing schedules for different databases (e.g., *FirstSearch* and *Dialog*)?

> Can the student articulate biases in information and describe nuances between objectivity and neutrality in authorities?[5]

Assignments

Many information issues already addressed in library instruction programs can be expanded and integrated into instruction and assignments for this indicator. These might include ethical contexts of intellectual property, equitable access to information, and fairness in media. Legal concerns include constitutional guarantees and institutional and national information policies, such as academic integrity, the Digital Millennium Copyright Act, and the USA PATRIOT Act. Socioeconomic areas could range from the dynamics of mass marketing in media and publishing to the impact of federal grant funding on the creation of knowledge. At a practical level, students' knowledge of this indicator can begin with an understanding of the role that the First Amendment's guarantee of freedom of speech plays in their academic explorations.

In their 2003 article, Hurlbert, Savidge, and Laudenslager offer an assignment that presents students with an "event happening on their campus that highlights basic rights of citizenship such as privacy (5.1.a) or free speech (5.1.c)." Students are then instructed to research these "rights" and apply the information they found to the campus event by writing an essay.[6]

The implications of current information policy should be discussed by students as users of public and private information and information delivery systems, as lifelong learners, and as informed citizens. The 2001 USA PATRIOT Act has broad implications for privacy, security, and civil liberties. It encompasses changes to over fifteen different statutes, including expanded provisions to make available information that was previously confidential and an increase in the penalties and scope of the Computer Fraud and Abuse Act.[7] Outcome 5.1.a addresses technological and information policy issues related to privacy and security of information use and access.

The Central Queensland University Library's online collection of assignments offer two assignments titled "Legislative Progression" and "Policy Progression." These exercises ask students to track a piece of legislation or policy though Parliament or Congress. They ask the questions, "Who are the organisations involved? What is the history of the issue? What are the ideological conflicts?" The authors believe that this will help students understand the processes of government and follow the politics and social implications of a critical issue.[8] To address performance indicator 5.1, this can focus on a specific piece of information policy.

In an effort to curb the rising cost of scholarly materials and authors' lack of control over their work products, many faculty and institutions are implementing exploratory solutions for the management of institutional scholarship, such as *Dspace*, the Massachusetts Institute of Technology Libraries' joint venture with Hewlett-Packard, and Ohio State University's *Knowledge Bank*. The development of institutional research data banks and repositories, as well as other alternatives to traditional scholarly publishing methods such as the initiatives of SPARC, the Scholarly Publishing and Academic Resources Coalition, will have increasing implications for student research. These complicated models and the economic context from which they arise must be introduced to the student researcher. Students must be able to analyze the information landscape to differentiate between information available free on the Internet and the types of resources accessible in vendor-delivered research databases available through their libraries (5.1.b). How often do we encounter a frustrated student who simply cannot understand why the website for the *Journal of Higher Education* does not yield the full text of the article he or she wants? Although a very reputable search tool led the student to what sounds like the perfect article, what's found is the table of contents for the journal issue and not the text of the article itself. The economics of information production greatly affects where scholarly and reputable information can be accessed. Students should be made aware that the changing information landscape makes available hybrid resource and research tools, where they may or may not be able to access the full text of articles and books for free.

University of Maryland University College's Information Literacy and Writing Assessment Project (ILWA Project) provides two additional applicable assignment examples. The lower-level assignments read as follows:

1. Have students explain what an information database is and how it is relevant for finding information.
2. Have students discuss the differences among various web search engines.[9]

Also provided are more advanced versions of these assignments, wherein students are asked to research a topic in a web search engine and subscription database, then compare and describe the resources available through the two tools, and finally discuss the similarities and differences between the tools.

Outcome 5.1.c asks students to analyze the broader context of research and publishing and identify the absence of, impeded access to, and censorship of particular ideas as applicable to their field of study. Such barriers may be social and professional as well as technological for students today. Miriam E. Joseph of Saint Louis University (Missouri) developed the following assignment to share alternative research ideas with the faculty. Her assignment suggests students browse the library stacks to examine book and journal titles in a specific discipline. The students should then write an essay in response to the following questions:

What is (discipline), i.e., how might it be defined?

How might the resources consulted be utilized in other courses, especially in other disciplines?

From this exercise, what have (you) learned about the scope of the discipline?[10]

UMUC's ILWA Project suggests the following:

1. Have students examine the role of information in a democratic society. What are the issues? How is information relevant or important to them?
2. Have students construct a timeline or map that illustrates the influence of a particular piece of published research and then summarize the relationship of the original research with what followed.[11]

Recording and sharing the processes and results of intellectual exploration is the foundation of the academic enterprise. Students who can successfully navigate this universe have developed some degree of understanding of how academics and other researchers create knowledge and of the impact that such information has on their own participation in the stream of intellectual exploration.

ASSESSING COMPLIANCE WITH INFORMATION POLICIES, LAWS, AND REGULATIONS

Performance Indicator 5.2. The information literate student follows laws, regulations, institutional policies, and etiquette related to the access and use of information resources.

> ***Outcome 5.2.a.*** Participates in electronic discussions following accepted practices (e.g., "Netiquette")
>
> ***Outcome 5.2.b.*** Uses approved passwords and other forms of ID for access to information resources
>
> ***Outcome 5.2.c.*** Complies with institutional policies on access to information resources
>
> ***Outcome 5.2.d.*** Preserves the integrity of information resources, equipment, systems, and facilities
>
> ***Outcome 5.2.e.*** Legally obtains, stores, and disseminates text, data, images, or sounds
>
> ***Outcome 5.2.g.*** Demonstrates an understanding of institutional policies related to human subjects research

This performance indicator asks students to demonstrate that they understand the rules and regulations surrounding information use by complying with policies and laws. Where the first performance indicator is constructive, asking students to develop and demonstrate knowledge, the second indicator is behavioral and prescriptive in nature. It asks students to comply (through their behavior) with regulations and adopt or internalize etiquette and values. With lawmakers considering using the criminal prosecution of individual students (rather than relying on campus policies) to deter the illegal trading of copyrighted material across campus networks, it is imperative that universities begin to address these issues more proactively with students.[12] Institutions must work to strike an acceptable balance between policy, the law, and personal and communal ethics. This begins with raising the consciousness and awareness of students and faculty through formal discussions of information use issues and institutional policies.

Central to the constitutional incarnation of copyright is the idea of promoting the development of scholarship through respect for the work of others. Performance indicator 5.2 asks students to work within and respect this environment. When students navigate, research, and create in the open universe of the World Wide Web, they should do so with the understanding that most of what they encounter is copyrighted, whether it carries stated authorship and copyright notice or not.

Article 1, Section 8 of the U.S. Constitution states: "Congress shall have the power . . . to promote the progress of sciences and useful arts, by securing for limited times to authors and inventors the exclusive rights to their respective writings and discoveries." Title 17, the copyright law of the U.S. Code, has expanded this original view greatly throughout the years. An author's rights now include the exclusive right to copy, distribute said copies, prepare derivative works, and perform and display a work publicly.

These rights do not remain pure, of course, and are open to negotiation, legal interpretation, and codified exemptions. The copyright world is, well, messy. With what was often seen as a moral right increasingly codified, authors and creators can parcel out their rights and sell portions off to publishers or whomever. Perhaps of greatest concern here is the fair use exemption, which allows the use of portions of copyrighted creative work in educational settings without first obtaining permission. Students and faculty must familiarize themselves with the parameters of this exemption in order to ethically and lawfully navigate the information universe of text, graphics, audio, and video. Congress set out "fair use" provisions that require an assessment for each individual use of a copyrighted work. There are numerous guidelines to help faculty and students stay "safely" within these provisions; some even specifically denote a suggested number of pages, stanzas, or seconds of a work that may be fairly used. A well-known example is the Fair Use Guidelines for Educational Multimedia by the Conference on Fair Use (CONFU).[13] These guidelines, including those of CONFU, are not legally binding, nor are they universally endorsed by professional associations and higher education institutions; they are just guidelines and are seen by some as safe harbors.

Such guidelines are often incorporated into library publications or codified as institutional policy. Judi Repman and Elizabeth Downs have outlined by policy type examples of items that may be used to develop policy provisions.[14] (See figure 7-1.)

Student Technology Use, Including Acceptable Use of Computers

- requirements for instruction in technology use such as an "Internet Driver's License"
- consequences of violating the Acceptable Use Policy
- use of multimedia hardware and software
- access to the Internet in the media center
- use of the Internet for research or recreational purposes
- appropriate use of technology during study hall, before and after school
- printing pages from the Internet for research or personal interest
- designing and posting websites on the school web server
- access to e-mail accounts, either through a school network or web e-mail services such as Hotmail

Faculty Technology Use, Including Acceptable Use of Computers

- requirements for instruction in technology and Internet use
- Internet access and use, including recreational surfing design and maintenance of class web pages
- use of e-mail accounts on school computers, either personal or through a school network

Copyright and New Technology Issues

- conducting software audits
- fair use issues, including fair use of multimedia and Internet information
- use of Internet filters
- regulations about posting school-related informational web pages
- use of media with distance learning technologies
- use of non-school-owned software on school computers
- use of CDs and videos from home on school-owned hardware

FIGURE 7-1
Examples of Policy Types

It would be appropriate to add to this table those policies guiding the use of copyrighted works and those prohibiting the piracy of software and other copyrighted material, as well as policies guiding student and faculty ownership of their own scholarship.

Many institutions have a range of information policies in place, and these should be reviewed regularly. Reviews should assess community needs as well as any pertinent changes in laws or regulations. To be effective, policies must be both widely disseminated and well understood within the campus community. The librarians, administrators, and faculty who design and implement information policy should ask themselves the following questions:

> Do students and faculty read fair use policies?
>
> When and where are students introduced to these campus policies?
>
> When are students introduced to copyright ownership policies?
>
> When are students introduced to technological use policies?
>
> Do faculty and administrative functions model and reinforce campus information policies?
>
> Do faculty respect the intellectual property of students and others in their own research and publication?

Unfortunately, students are more likely to be informed, through student computer labs and campus e-mail services, of their institutions' appropriate computing policies than of copyright and fair use. It is possible that well-informed students, who possess an understanding of themselves as the creators and owners of intellectual property, may adopt more ethical practices as consumers of both scholarly and popular information.

Assessment Queries

The following three queries from the same instrument assess a student's knowledge of policies and procedures in the use of and access to information (5.2.b–f):[15]

> What disciplinary action might happen to community college students who violate the policies on plagiarism? (short answer required)
>
> To gain access to your college library's online databases from *off campus* you would (short answer required)

You must create a radio advertisement for your job. You want to use a small part of a popular song from a CD for background music. What is required of you, if anything, before broadcasting this advertisement?

    a. Notify the songwriter that you will use part of his song.

    b. Find out who distributed the song and negotiate with them for the right to play part of this song.

    c. Nothing; you can use the song since you are only playing a small part of it.

    d. You can use the song since you paid for the CD it is published on.

The Wartburg College (Iowa) *Information Literacy Pre-Test for IS 201* mapped the next two questions to the outcomes in assessing students' knowledge of online discussion practices (5.2.a) and specific campus policy provisions (5.2.c), respectively:

Why should one never type an e-mail in all caps?

    a. It is "shouting" and a breach of netiquette.

    b. It is hard on the keyboard.

    c. It is hard on the eyes.

    d. It is culturally offensive for some.

Each of these actions is a violation of the Wartburg Computing Policy as outlined in the Student Handbook (true or false):

    Creating and posting my own page on the Wartburg server with authorization

    Sharing my ID with my roommate

    Accessing the Wartburg Information Network from off campus

    Downloading MP3 files

Assignments

The C©pyrightsite.org website, developed by Vivian Wright and colleagues in the College of Education at the University of Alabama, offers sample assignments that teach directly to a specific issue involving copyright. For example, "Using/Not Using Copyrighted Information" (a small-group assignment)

requires students to build a multimedia presentation (web page or Power-Point presentation) to teach particular subject matter or address an assigned research problem that uses third-party copyrighted material.[16] To address outcomes 5.2.d and 5.2.e, the students are to incorporate texts, images, and sounds as appropriate and actively seek permissions when necessary. The faculty member must make sure that students approach this assignment with a working knowledge of the concepts of copyright and fair use and that they understand when it is necessary and how to seek permissions. It is likely that students will need to be given guides for reference. Unlike other general assignments covering the issue of copyright, these assignments teach very specific concepts, such as "contributory infringement and Internet service providers" and "deep linking"—areas of the U.S. copyright law that are currently being formed.[17]

A similar assignment from Austen Peay State University (Tennessee) is titled "Web Site and Web Portfolio Project." In this assignment students build a website, research and evaluate material for content, and apply their knowledge of fair use and copyright laws for a freely available public website. Although this assignment was used for a graduate course, it can easily be adapted for undergraduates. It involves the application of multiple aspects of information literacy, including Standard 5 and its outcomes.[18]

An introduction to the previous assignment can be accomplished with an assignment developed by Sheryl Hinman in which students are required to investigate the use of a celebrity's public image and intellectual property. In small teams, students check websites for copyright violations (5.1.d), assess the attribution of elements on the sites (5.3.b), work to determine if all the use of copyrighted material is within the parameters of fair use where applicable (5.1.d), and identify any original content in the sites and any other materials that don't need permission (5.2.f).[19]

The ACRL's Information Literacy website includes an effective scenario to address outcome 5.2.b in "The Standards Step-by-Step: Standard Five":

> Students receive passwords and other forms of ID on a regular basis. Have them identify how many they have and ask them to reflect on the reasons for restricted access.[20]

This can be supplemented with other queries such as: Are there challenges in conforming to set regulations? What are the benefits or challenges in having this access or privilege? Do you give up freedoms by participating in these systems of knowledge and information management?

An additional scenario to address outcomes 5.2.c and 5.2.d would be:

> A student captures a film clip used in an online course and uploads it to a peer-to-peer file-sharing network. Discuss the information issues involved. What policies or laws are involved?

ASSESSING ACADEMIC INTEGRITY, PLAGIARISM, AND SCHOLARLY ACCOUNTABILITY

Performance Indicator 5.3. The information literate student acknowledges the use of information sources in communicating the product or performance.

> ***Outcome 5.3.a.*** Selects an appropriate documentation style and uses it consistently to cite sources
>
> ***Outcome 5.3.b.*** Posts permission granted notices, as needed, for copyrighted material
>
> ***Outcome 5.2.f.*** Demonstrates an understanding of what constitutes plagiarism and does not represent work attributable to others as his/her own

Performance indicator 5.3 and outcome 5.2.f each address the concept of plagiarism and academic integrity. Studies throughout the 1990s, and most recently in 2002, present a high percentage (up to 90 percent) of students self-reporting having cheated at some time during their academic careers.[21] Clearly this is a situation that needs to be addressed. Educators are left with the question: What is our role in addressing the current reality of increased information access and the changing paradigm of how the student researcher interacts with information and the system of academic knowledge production?

Assessment Queries

Results by a host of researchers over the past thirty years have essentially confirmed either a "significant" occurrence or a rise in self-reported/perceived academic dishonesty by students. Many of these survey queries addressed the contextual and personal factors involved in academic dishonesty, as listed below:

Relationship of field of study, discipline, academic level, or gender to occurrence[22]

Application of the honor code concept in face-to-face and distance education classrooms—traditional, modified, and no codes (no unproctored exams, no pledge, no rat clause)[23]

Student's perception of peer behavior[24]

Student's perception of the likelihood of policy enforcement[25]

Student's perception of the severity of punishment[26]

Number of cases pursued by faculty[27]

Student's perception of an instructor's ethics[28]

Student's institutional and disciplinary ethics[29]

Personal indicators as cause (time, grade pressure, moral code/values, etc.)[30]

The Center for Intellectual Property at University of Maryland University College is currently surveying 2,500 distance educators, faculty, and academic administrators at selected "asynchronous learning network" institutions across the United States to ascertain their perceptions of student behavior, identify best practices on the institutional level, and provide further information to students and faculty on how to address academic integrity issues in the online classroom. The project will also study student use of digital content and faculty use of digital methods to detect plagiarism.[31] This current research will contribute to the body of literature on student academic dishonesty, which has had a clear impact on both pedagogy and policy.

In addition to contextual and personal indicators, a thorough assessment of performance indicator 5.3 should include assessing students' understanding of the concepts of plagiarism and intellectual dishonesty and their demonstration of that understanding in their own writing. For this performance indicator, self-perception and behavior queries could include:

How often do you cut and paste text from an Internet source without acknowledging the author?

Do you believe other students submit papers purchased from term paper mills for a grade?

Queries to directly test students' understanding could include:

Is this an example of proper use?

Is this an example of plagiarism? or, What is plagiarism?[32]

What is a bibliography?

Why do bibliographies accompany most academic writing?

Queries that assess students' application of their understanding within their own assignments include:

Do the students properly cite resources in the text of their written products?

Are the students able to discuss the relationship of citations to other information sources?[33]

Do the students indicate what was easy to find, what was not, and why (by means of a research log or journal)?

Do the students acknowledge related information sources?

The *UMBC Survey* poses the following query, which assesses a student's basic knowledge of the performance indicator and outcomes outlined in this section, when working with written text:

Suppose you are writing a research paper and you read an article on your topic. In which of the following instances would you cite the material as a footnote/endnote/reference in your paper? Please check all that apply.

a. When you copy a whole paragraph

b. When you write it over in your own words

c. When you quote one sentence from the article, using quotation marks

d. None of the above

e. All of the above

f. I don't know

Several instruments reviewed posed a question that asked students to identify whether a given citation or list of citations corresponded to a book, journal article, magazine article, government document, web page, and so on. These types of queries test a student's aptitude beyond a basic definition of citation or bibliography. A more advanced version of this type of assessment could be integrated with an assignment:

Write a complete bibliographic citation for the three sources you selected using a standard citation format, indicating which format (MLA, APA, CBE) you used.

Assignments

Many institutions have developed diverse avenues and methods to teach about the issue of plagiarism and foster academic integrity. One of the wonderful things about this topic is that you can typically find it being addressed at all levels of the institution. Among the methods used by librarians, individual faculty, academic departments, and campuswide initiatives are:

Workshops (writing centers, libraries, freshmen seminars, new student orientations)

Online guides, tutorials, and campus information clearinghouses (writing centers, libraries, honor councils, and judiciary boards)

In-class discussions (faculty)

In-class overviews and guides (faculty)

Student handbooks and policies (student services, academic deans, departmental chairs, faculty)

Brochures (student services, libraries, honor councils, and judiciary boards)

Bookmarks, mugs, pencils, and other novelty reminders (student services, libraries)

Educational video clips (student services, libraries, honor councils, and judiciary boards)

Plagiarism detection tools, services, and software (faculty, writing centers, libraries)

Fostering a sense of community is said to be one of the greatest challenges in online and distance education. If academic integrity is to be part of the values of a community, educators must work to creatively encourage student investment by providing forums in both virtual and face-to-face classrooms for student discussion. McCabe, Trevino and Butterfield warn that "schools that do not engage their students in a meaningful dialog about academic integrity are likely to experience the persistent levels of academic dishonesty identified in virtually all research on cheating in college."[34]

Kenneth D. Pimple of Indiana University uses the case study method as an effective way to engage students in a discussion of ethics in research and specific academic disciplines. He suggests beginning with a set of ground rules for discussion and guiding the initial direction of the discussion. For example, if given a scenario in which a character named Carol Peterson is confronted by her instructor because of suspected plagiarism, the students in the course could be asked to:

> Decide which of the two positions to defend: Should Peterson copy the notes? Why or why not?
>
> Solve a problem: What should Peterson do?
>
> Take a role: What would you do if you were Peterson? Her instructor? The dean?
>
> Think about how the problem could have been avoided: What went wrong here?

Pimple's article goes on to present specific procedural details involved in presenting this type of exercise to students.[35]

Common approaches to developing plagiarism-resistant assignments include having students focus on analysis and the process of research rather than on the end product. Examples of these assignments abound. Hurlbert, Savidge, and Laudenslager of Lycoming College (Pennsylvania) define "process-based design" as applying to "single projects, a series of assignments throughout the semester, or the total of assignments developed for a particular curriculum."[36] Faculty have found that occurrences of plagiarism are reduced when students are required to report at several stages of their research process verbally or in research logs and journals. This type of assignment and reflective assessment allows the students and the instructors to assess their knowledge development. Specifically, the research log or journal allows students to practice the mechanics of proper in-text and bibliographic citations, paraphrasing, and summarizing.

A final assignment example could be accomplished in a library instruction session as well as a formal class session:

> Take a text. Go through it with a class and pull out a quotable phrase. Talk about the elements included in a bibliographic citation and outline them. Construct a proper in-text reference and bibliography/works cited reference. Discuss proper and improper ways of incorporating this into a writing assignment.

NOTES

1. See Angela Congrove, Otterbein College, "Survey of College Students regarding Copyright Law Information" (2004), http://www.otterbein.edu/surveys/copyright.

2. Jeremy J. Shapiro and Shelley K. Hughes, "Information Literacy as a Liberal Art," *Educom Review* 31, no. 2 (1996): 31–35.

3. Cushla Kapitzke, "Information Literacy: A Positivist Epistemology and a Politics of *Out*formation," *Educational Theory* 53, no. 1 (Winter 2003): 37–53.

4. Carol Boston, "The Concept of Formative Assessment," *Practical Assessment, Research and Evaluation* 8, no. 9 (2002), http://pareonline.net/getvn.asp?v=8&n=9/.

5. Patricia Daragan and Gwendolyn Stevens, "Developing Lifelong Learners: An Integrative and Developmental Approach to Information Literacy," *Research Strategies* 14, no. 2 (1996): 68–81.

6. Janet McNeil Hurlbert, Cathleen R. Savidge, and Georgia R. Laudenslager, "Process-Based Assignments: How Promoting Information Literacy Prevents Plagiarism," *College and Undergraduate Libraries* 10, no. 1 (2003): 39–51.

7. *USA PATRIOT Act*, Public Law 107-56, 107th Cong. On February 3, 2006, the presdident signed into law H. R. 4659, which extends certain provisions of the *USA PATRIOT Act* to March 10, 2006; http://www.whitehouse.gov/news/releases/2006/02/20060203-16.html.

8. Central Queensland University Library, "Assessment Ideas," http://www.library.cqu.edu.au/informationliteracy/teachresources/ assess_list.htm.

9. Kimberly E. Kelley, Information and Library Services, University of Maryland University College, "Information Literacy and Writing Assessment Project: Tutorial for Developing and Evaluating Assignments," http://www.umuc.edu/library/tutorials/information_literacy/sect4.html#sample.

10. Miriam E. Joseph, Pius XII Memorial Library, Saint Louis University, "Term Paper Alternatives or . . . So You'd Like Your Students to Use the Library but Don't Want to Assign a Research Paper?" (1992), http://www.lib.berkeley.edu/TeachingLib/PaperAlternatives.html.

11. Kelley, "Information Literacy and Writing Assessment Project."

12. Andrea L. Foster, "Lawmakers Demand That Colleges Crack Down on Illegal File Sharing," *Chronicle of Higher Education*, Information Technology, February 27, 2003, http://chronicle.com/free/ 2003/02/2003022701t.htm.

13. Educational Multimedia Fair Use Guidelines Development Committee, "Fair Use Guidelines for Educational Multimedia, Central Michigan University" (1996), http://www.oit.cmich.edu/it/policies_multi_fairuse.asp.

14. Judi Repman and Elizabeth Downs, "Policy Issues for the 21st Century Library Media Center," *Book Report* 17, no. 5 (March/April 1999): 8–11. Permission for reprinting this table granted by *Library Media Connection* and the authors.

15. Bay Area Community Colleges Assessment Project Team, *Bay Area Community Colleges Assessment Project: A Two-Part Information Competency Assessment Exam*, http://www.topsy.org/ICAP/ICAProject.html. The Bay Area Community Colleges Assessment

Project Team includes Bonnie Gratch-Lindauer, project leader, Pam Baker, Amelie Brown, Micca Gray, Andy Kivel, Brian Lym, and Topsy Smalley.

16. Vivian Wright, College of Education, University of Alabama, "The C©pyrightsite," http://www.thecopyrightsite.org/.

17. For an example of the academic climate that necessitates these types of assignments, see Kelley McCollum and Peter Schmidt, "How Forcefully Should Universities Enforce Copyright Law on Audio Files?" *Chronicle of Higher Education* 46, no. 13 (1999): A59–60.

18. Lori Buchanan, Ted Jones, and DeAnne Luck, Austin Peay State University, "Collaborating Online to Teach Information and Multimedia Literacy," paper presented at the Seventh Annual Mid-South Instructional Technology Conference, "Teaching, Learning, and Technology: The Connected Classroom," Murfreesboro, TN, April 7–9, 2002, http://www.mtsu.edu/~itconf/proceed02/50.html.

19. Sheryl Hinman, "Analyzing Copyright in the Technology World," *Update on Law-Related Education* 22, no. 2 (1998): 46–50.

20. Association of College and Research Libraries, "Information Literacy: The Standards Step-by-Step: Standard Five," http://www.ala.org/ala/acrl/acrlissues/acrlinfolit/infolitstandards/stepbystep1/stepbystep.htm#standard5.

21. See Donald McCabe, Linda Klebe Trevino, and Kenneth D. Butterfield, "Cheating in Academic Institutions: A Decade of Research," *Ethics and Behavior* 11, no. 3 (2001): 219–33; Donald McCabe and Linda Klebe Trevino, "Individual and Contextual Influences on Academic Dishonesty: A Multicampus Investigation," *Research in Higher Education* 38, no. 3 (1997): 379–97; Donald L. McCabe, "Faculty Responses to Academic Dishonesty: The Influence of Student Honor Codes," *Research in Higher Education* 34, no. 5 (1993): 647–59; and Patrick M. Scanlon and David R. Neumann, "Internet Plagiarism among College Students," *Journal of College Student Development* 43 (2002): 374–85.

22. Jonah Allen Ward, "University Students' Views regarding Academic Dishonesty in Two Disciplines" (Ph.D. diss., University of Miami, 1998); Ethel Francine Plusquellic Roberts, "Faculty Perceptions of Baccalaureate Nursing Students' Unethical Behavior and the Implications for the Curriculum and Profession" (Ph.D. diss., George Mason University, 1996); D. A. Ward and W. L. Beck, "Gender and Dishonesty," *Journal of Social Psychology* 130, no. 3 (1990): 333–39.

23. Donald McCabe, Linda Klebe Trevino, and Kenneth D. Butterfield, "Dishonesty in Academic Environments: The Influence of Peer Reporting Requirements," *Journal of Higher Education* 72, no. 1 (2001): 29–45; Donald McCabe and Patrick Drinan, "Toward a Culture of Academic Integrity," *Chronicle of Higher Education* 46, no. 8 (1999): B7; Donald McCabe, Linda Klebe Trevino, and Kenneth D. Butterfield, "Academic Integrity in Honor Code and Non-Honor Code Environments," *Journal of Higher Education* 70, no. 2 (1999): 211–35.

24. Scanlon and Neumann, "Internet Plagiarism among College Students."

25. McCabe, "Faculty Responses to Academic Dishonesty"; Deborah F. Crown and M. Shane Spiller, "Learning from the Literature on Collegiate Cheating: A Review of Empirical Research," *Journal of Business Ethics* 17 (1998): 383–90.

26. Crown and Spiller, "Learning from the Literature on Collegiate Cheating"; D. A. Ward and J. Nantel, "Deterrence or Labeling: The Effect of Informal Sanctions," *Deviant Behavior: An Inter Disciplinary Journal* 14 (1993): 43–64.

27. Crown and Spiller, "Learning from the Literature on Collegiate Cheating."

28. Melissa Ann Manning, "Cheating, Anomie and Academic Ethics" (Ph.D. diss., University of Kansas, 1994).

29. Manning, "Cheating, Anomie and Academic Ethics"; Roberts, "Faculty Perceptions of Baccalaureate Nursing Students' Unethical Behavior."

30. Arlene Franklyn-Stokes and Stephen E. Newstead, "Undergraduate Cheating: Who Does What and Why," *Studies in Higher Education* 20, no. 2 (June 1995): 159–72; McCabe and Trevino, "Individual and Contextual Influences on Academic Dishonesty"; Chris Park, "In Other (People's) Words: Plagiarism by University Students—Literature and Lessons," *Assessment and Evaluation in Higher Education* 28, no. 5 (2003): 471–88.

31. University of Maryland University College, Center for Intellectual Property and Copyright, "Faculty and Administrator Perceptions of Academic Integrity: A Survey" (2003), http://www.umuc.edu/distance/odell/cip/research.html.

32. Researchers from many disciplines continue to interrogate the origins and parameters of the term "plagiarism" and the concept of "academic dishonesty." Before constructing a survey question, you may want to investigate the work of the following authors: Miguel Roig, "Can Undergraduate Students Determine Whether Text Has Been Plagiarized?" *Psychological Record* 47, no. 1 (1997): 113–22; M. K. Johnson, S. Hastroudi, and D. S. Lindsay, "Source Monitoring," *Psychological Bulletin* 114, no. 3 (1993): 3–28; A. L. Betz, John J. Skowronski, and Thomas M. Ostrom, "Shared Realities: Social Influence and Stimulus Memory," *Social Cognition* 14, no. 2 (1996): 113–14; C. Neil Macrae, Galen V. Bodenhausen, and Guglielmo Calvini, "Contexts of Cryptomnesia: May the Source Be with You," *Social Cognition* 17 (1999): 273–97; Rebecca Moore Howard, *Standing in the Shadow of Giants: Plagiarists, Authors, Collaborators* (Stamford, CT: Ablex, 1999); Rebecca Moore Howard, "Plagiarisms, Authorships, and the Academic Death Penalty," *College English* 57, no. 7 (1995): 788–806; and Alastair Pennycook, "Borrowing Others' Words: Text, Ownership, Memory, and Plagiarism," *TESOL Quarterly* 30, no. 2 (1996): 201–30.

33. Indiana University Bloomington Libraries, Assessment Planning Committee, "An Assessment Plan for Information Literacy (Final)", 1996, http://www.indiana.edu/~libinstr/Information_Literacy/assessment.html.

34. McCabe, Trevino, and Butterfield, "Cheating in Academic Institutions."

35. Kenneth D. Pimple, "Using Case Studies in Teaching Research Ethics" (2003), http://poynter.indiana.edu/tre/kdp-cases.pdf.

36. Hurlbert, Savidge and Laudenslager, "Process-Based Assignments."

Beyond the Standards:
What Now?

Teresa Y. Neely

T his chapter will discuss areas that should be considered in information literacy assessment but are not covered by the ACRL Standards. The nature of the relationship between students and faculty, students' perceptions of and attitudes about the standards, detailed demographic and background information on student populations with regard to information literacy, and students' technological competencies are often overlooked in information literacy assessment. However, these areas are critical to the overall process in determining students' preparedness and information literacy exposure. Examples of assessment questions for these areas are also included in this chapter.

Of the four areas addressed, students' relationship with faculty is usually the most overlooked element in library-related instruction in general. Demographics are almost always included in assessment, but the analysis of many of the components is usually descriptive and limited. Technological competence is critical in order for college-level students to participate and succeed in academia and the workforce. The inclusion of questions in these areas is strongly recommended in order to enhance and improve your assessment endeavors.

STUDENTS' RELATIONSHIP WITH FACULTY

In her 2000 dissertation research findings, Teresa Y. Neely's statistical analysis of the sociological and psychological factors that contribute to a student's ability to make relevance judgments revealed that the student's relationship with the faculty is generally the most overlooked factor in library and information literacy assessment. "As a function of how students acquire information literacy and library research skills and their attitudes about these skills, the student/faculty relationship is an important aspect at all levels of the academe."[1]

Neely's research confirmed that faculty generally "expect students at all levels to possess the research and information literacy skills in order to complete assignments and research projects and in doing so, structure class assignments and coursework accordingly."[2] However, research shows that students' relationship with faculty indirectly affects the students' performance (when tested on information literacy skills) and attitude (how they feel about information literacy skills). This is so because their relationship with faculty affects students' exposure (to the library/information science environment) and their experience (within the library/information science environment).[3] Simply put, faculty are key; students become exposed and experienced through their relationship with the faculty.

Although the ACRL Standards only mention the word *instructor* once throughout the entire document (see outcome 1.1.a), the importance of this aspect of information literacy cannot and should not be underestimated. Additionally, the context of this mention in Standard 1 focuses on the student "conferring with instructors" to define and articulate an information need. Statistically, it has been proven that students' relationship with the faculty affects their attitudes about and performance levels with information literacy skills.[4] Clearly this is a critical relationship because it involves the faculty introducing information literacy skills to students, modeling the use and mastery of these skills, and integrating them into the curriculum. The faculty are powerfully important in developing information-literate college students and in promoting lifelong learning and an information-literate citizenry.

Assessment Queries

The *Neely Test* includes seven items designed to glean more information about the nature of the relationships students might have with faculty members during their academic careers. The relationships were defined as either advisor/advisee (primarily graduate students) or classroom interaction (primarily undergraduate students).

One question inquires about the number of faculty members who have encouraged the use of information resources in a variety of formats. Another question, which also appears in the *UMBC Survey*, asks students about their experience(s) in the classroom and in completing course work:

> In responding to this question, please consider your experience with faculty in completing required assignments for courses. Please select all that apply.
>
> a. Faculty member requires no use of outside material for completing course assignments.
>
> b. Faculty member requires use of only lectures and assigned textbook(s) for completing course assignments.
>
> c. Faculty member requires use of library to retrieve reserve materials.
>
> d. Faculty member makes use of library materials (print and/or electronic) when presenting course material and lectures.
>
> e. Faculty member requires or suggests use of library materials (print and/or electronic) when assigning course work.
>
> f. Faculty member invites librarians to introduce course-related library materials (print and/or electronic).

Responses to this query, along with specific academic department-related demographics, could provide key information about which departments or individual faculty members are referring students to the library and modeling positive information-literate behavior by recommending resources. A drawback to this query is that it does not reveal specific recommended resources. Students who receive a list of recommended journal titles from a faculty member could list that occurrence as a faculty member encouraging the use of library materials; but if the library does not own or no longer subscribes to the titles listed, is it really modeling positive information-literate behavior? Follow-up questions could be developed to ask students about the types of resources faculty have referred them to and if they felt the resources helped them in their research.

Another query from the *UMBC Survey* focuses on whether faculty members provide opportunities for students to be exposed to an information-literate environment.

> Has a faculty member done any of the following? Please select all that apply.
>
> a. Referred you to a specific librarian
>
> b. Encouraged you to seek a librarian's assistance

    c. Taken your class to the library for a librarian-led tour/orientation

    d. Taken your class to the library for one or more instruction sessions in the library and/or classroom

    e. None of the above

Several of the questions from the *Neely Test* focus specifically on the nature of the relationship itself. Students are asked if they have participated in any one-on-one-type relationships with faculty: independent study or research or teaching practicum. Students who respond positively are queried further on the nature of the relationship. The question that follows is presented to students who responded positively to:

> Have you participated in an independent study/student-initiated research under consultation with faculty member(s) [includes research papers, thesis, dissertation]? (yes/no)

> If yes, please describe the nature of the relationship. Select all that apply.
>
>   a. Faculty made him/herself available for regular meetings and provided helpful feedback and required progress reports.
>
>   b. Faculty was knowledgeable about deadlines and departmental guidelines.
>
>   c. Faculty kept me informed about matters related to my academic well-being.
>
>   d. Faculty provided guidance and assistance in accessing resources (print and online) in conducting literature reviews.
>
>   e. Faculty often did not have time to meet with me to discuss my work.

> Have you participated in directed research/teaching practicum with faculty member(s) [includes participating in research project or (co)teaching a course(s) designed by faculty]? (yes/no)

> If yes, please describe the nature of the relationship. Select all that apply.
>
>   a. Faculty member(s) treated me respectfully as a junior colleague.
>
>   b. Faculty member(s) treated me as a gopher and student help.

    c. Faculty provided constructive criticism and feedback on project/teaching effort.

    d. Faculty often did not have time to meet with me to discuss my work.

An additional question inquires about how the relationship(s) began.

In view of the type of relationships described in the items above, please indicate how the relationship started. Select all that apply.

    a. No relationship of this type with faculty.

    b. Faculty was highly regarded in subject area of interest.

    c. Had prior relationship with faculty member.

    d. Faculty member was recommended/assigned by the department.

    e. Faculty member was recommended by other students/faculty.

    f. Faculty invited me to participate in research project/teaching course.

The addition of queries that provide insight and useful data on faculty members' interaction with students is strongly recommended. Clearly, these types of queries can provide rich data about teaching faculty and their commitment to information literacy skills integration into their classrooms and the curriculum.

ATTITUDINAL DATA

The majority of assessment efforts do not consider students' perceptions or attitudes about the concepts on which they are being tested. Students' attitudes are important at every stage of the educational process, however. They are especially critical in terms of library instruction, the library in general, using computers, and library and information literacy–related anxiety. Researchers must be careful that they do not make decisions based solely on students' self-reported attitudes. College-level students tend to overestimate their skill set and express overconfidence with individual skills. However, when asked to demonstrate those individual skills, they fail to do so at the same levels.[5] It is also important to know whether students deem a skill important or if they feel that a particular skill is actually a skill or more of a mind-set. For example, Heather Morrison's 1997 research revealed that those participating in a focus group disagreed about whether "recognizing a need for information" was really a skill.[6] By not asking students how they feel, researchers do not have an overall picture of their student population.

Assessment Queries

Many of the surveys reviewed for this book included questions that asked students to report their comfort or confidence levels with library research skills. However, prior to the *Neely Test*, with the exception of a 1997 study, there was very little evidence that students had been asked how they felt about information literacy skills.[7] Although the *Neely Test* was developed prior to the publication of the ACRL Standards, students taking the *Neely Test* were asked to respond to ten skills that closely resemble the standards. These skills were taken from Christina S. Doyle's 1992 dissertation research.[8] For the first two skills, students responded to a five-scale Likert-type query (strongly agree, agree, undecided/neutral, disagree, strongly disagree):

> I recognize that accurate and complete information is the basis for intelligent decision making.

> When faced with a problem in daily life (school-related, work-related, in general), I generally try to find information as the first step in solving the problem.

The latter part of the question required students to indicate their comfort levels (very comfortable, comfortable, undecided/neutral, uncomfortable, very uncomfortable) with the remaining skills:

> Formulating questions based on information needs

> Identifying potential sources of information

> Developing successful search strategies

> Accessing sources of information including computer-based and other technologies

> Evaluating information

> Organizing information for practical application

> Integrating new information into an existing body of knowledge

> Using information in critical thinking and problem solving

Additional areas for attitudinal research include how students feel about computers and libraries (anxiety), conducting research, and interacting with librarians. Exploring students' confidence and comfort levels on different aspects of libraries and the research environment may also be beneficial. Because the profession has embraced the ACRL Standards, it is hoped that future information literacy assessment instruments will include an attitudinal component in order to build a body of research-based literature that accurately characterizes college-level students' attitudes about these important skills.

DEMOGRAPHIC DATA

In addition to the demographics that are commonly gathered during information literacy assessment such as academic status, age, and major, it is a good idea to gather more detailed demographic data in order to provide an accurate profile of the student population you are assessing. For assessment at the University of Maryland, Baltimore County, the following data were deemed important for data analysis and for providing a holistic demographic profile of the student population.

Gender. There is empirical evidence that there are gender differences in some aspects of information literacy skills assessment.[9] This is a demographic that is commonly included, but the body of research on this particular element is more descriptive than statistically relevant.

Birth date. This element is important if you are attempting to determine if your population includes traditional- or nontraditional-age students. The literature reveals that nontraditional-age adults have different learning styles than traditional-age college-level students and thus may require different assessment and instructional approaches.[10]

Ethnic heritage and race. There is virtually no research on whether the ethnicity or race of college-level students is a factor in information literacy skills assessment and development. The acquisition of and subsequent statistical analysis of data would provide some insight into whether this aspect of the "digital divide" is really an issue to be addressed within the information literacy framework.[11]

Country of citizenship; country of birth. Students who learn to use the library in countries other than the United States or in primarily non-English-speaking countries may not have the same exposure to or experience with library and information science environments as students in the United

States. It is helpful to know as much as possible about the background of students in your population in order to interpret the results correctly and to develop intervention strategies and information literacy programs that meet the needs of all students at your institution.

Native language. Students who are nonnative English speakers, or for whom English is a second or third language, may not perform well on an English survey using English idioms, acronyms, or jargon. In terms of analyzing data, this element may provide some insight into questions that may need to be revised.

High school. High school and other secondary library environments vary greatly. The background and experiences in libraries and research environments of students enrolling in colleges is wide and disparate. For example, if students have not been exposed to an OPAC, they cannot be expected to perform well on queries about an OPAC, especially if they do not understand the question or cannot determine what the acronym means. It might be helpful to include queries that ask students about their experiences in secondary school libraries. Additionally, high school geographic data may assist in the analysis of the overall demographic makeup of your population.

Colleges and universities attended. Students who have attended other colleges or universities may have been exposed to a more or less stringent information literacy program or program of instruction. It is important to know who may have been exposed and in what environment (community college, research university) in order to develop a program that allows students the flexibility to acquire basic skills or to build on higher-order skills already introduced and acquired elsewhere.

Most surveys place the demographic section at the beginning of the survey in order to inspire participants' confidence levels. There is also the theory that placing these questions at the end of the survey will inspire positive feelings of accomplishment in the participants. These types of queries can be instrumental in lengthening surveys. It is advisable to identify alternative ways to obtain demographic data other than developing queries. For example, librarians at the University of Maryland, Baltimore County, partnered with the school's Office of Information Technology and were successful in implementing the *UMBC Survey* via the campus portal, my.UMBC.edu. Students were presented with the survey as one of the options when they logged in to their UMBC accounts. Researchers then had access to detailed demographic data from the student data system that stores the data obtained from student applications. Confidentiality was maintained because upon authentication, students only transmitted a unique user name along with their responses to the survey and no other identifying information.

TECHNOLOGICAL COMPETENCIES

The impact of technology on higher education is becoming more and more significant. Technology has permeated all aspects of the learning environment, and faculty and students must be technologically proficient in order to be successful. For example, in order to register for classes, access grades, and pay tuition, students have to acquire and master certain basic technology skills. In order to be successful academically, they must be able to access, retrieve, evaluate, manage, and use information effectively and efficiently from a variety of print and nonprint sources. Information resources are multiplying exponentially and are becoming more diverse, more complex, and more interdisciplinary. Successful students must be information literate, as well as technologically proficient, in order to complete basic course work and degree requirements.[12]

Faculty and staff are increasingly required to master technology to do their jobs on a daily basis. Additionally, faculty are often rewarded for integrating technology into their courses. The effects of this transition/migration can be most significantly felt in the classroom. Faculty are increasingly making use of portals to customize their access to information resources as well as to provide access to course materials for their students. Utilizing course management software such as WebCT or Blackboard enables faculty to provide greater access to students, as well as to encourage creativity and critical thinking by making use of the software's interactive functions and to create and foster an enhanced online environment.[13]

Assessment Queries

The ACRL Standards do not specifically focus on technological competency, but a certain level of competency is presumed in order to complete the tasks described in the outcomes: using electronic discussions (1.1.a, 3.6.b–c, 5.2.a); selecting information retrieval systems, implementing searches, retrieving information online, and selecting from various technologies to extract, record, and manage information (2); using computer and other technologies to study the interaction of ideas and other phenomena (3.3.c); manipulating digital text, images, and data (4.1.d); using a range of information technology applications

(4.3.b); and understanding issues of privacy and security in electronic environments (5.1.a).

Very few of the survey instruments reviewed contained queries designed to independently assess students' technology competency levels. Of those identified, the majority of them were designed to elicit self-reported levels of competency with individual tasks or skills. The responses to these laundry-list types of assessments may not provide usable data unless results are analyzed in conjunction with data that demonstrate competence, but the detail in these lists can be used to develop related queries that do require students to demonstrate knowledge and competency levels.[14] Other types of technology questions identified were closed-end, requiring yes/no or true/false responses:

> Do you use e-mail? (yes/no)
>
> Do you use the World Wide Web/Internet? (yes/no)
>
> Do you have off-campus access to the campus network? (yes/no)
>
> The Internet is the same thing as the World Wide Web. (true/false)

As noted previously, questions such as these do not provide data on whether or not a student is proficient at using e-mail, navigating the World Wide Web, or accessing the campus network from a distance. Asking students questions with specific options for them to select provides more informative data. Librarians at Colorado State University developed the *CSU Minimum Competency Survey* to test the competency levels of faculty and staff working in an information commons environment. The question below could be revised to ask what e-mail accounts students use primarily or to assess students' knowledge of a variety of technologies; for example, the types of online courseware used at a particular institution (Blackboard, WebCT, etc.).

> What e-mail accounts can be read using Webmail?
>
> _____ Excite _____ Hotmail
>
> _____ Lamar _____ Yahoo
>
> _____ AOL _____ Holly
>
> _____ Manta

In 1991 researchers at Cornell University conducted a survey of business and finance graduates, *Computer Skills for Information Retrieval and Management: A Survey of the Skills of Selected Cornell University Business and Finance Graduates (Cornell Computer Skills Survey)*. It included a query similar to the one above, asking graduates what type of computers they used.

Another query from the *Cornell Computer Skills Survey* asked graduates to assess their computer skills in reference to their jobs. This query could be adapted to assess students' perceptions of the computing skills required for the courses they are taking in their majors. This type of query could also provide students with an option to evaluate their computer skills for assignments and course requirements, as well as to compare their skill set to those of their colleagues.

> How important were your computing skills to being hired for your job?

>> a. My computer skills were very important for the job; only candidates with appropriate skills were considered.

>> b. My computer skills were important for the job; candidates with these skills had an advantage over candidates without these skills.

>> c. My computer skills were somewhat important for the job; it was preferred that candidates have these skills, but candidates with or without them were eligible for hire.

>> d. My computer skills were not important for the job and they were not a factor in my being hired; candidates with or without these skills were qualified for hiring.

In terms of determining a student's familiarity with technology unique to your institution, the following question from the *CSU Minimum Competency Survey* can be adapted accordingly. The additional questions that follow, from the same instrument, can be adapted to require students to demonstrate their knowledge of and proficiency with other aspects of technology.

> Which plug-in does the Libraries Data Game use?

> _____ Adobe Acrobat Reader

> _____ Authorware

> _____ Quick Time

> _____ Real Player

> _____ I don't know

Which of these three buttons would you use to maximize a window?

_____ _____ _____ I don't know _____

How do you get to Task Manager (to allow you to shut down programs that are not responding)? Select all that apply.

_____ press Control, Alt, Delete simultaneously

_____ right click on the Task Bar and choose Task Manager

_____ right click on the Desktop and choose Properties

_____ turn off/reset the computer

_____ I don't know

Which of the following would *not* work to move a file or folder? Select all that apply.

_____ a. highlight the file/folder and use the arrow key to move it over

_____ b. cut and paste

_____ c. drag and drop

_____ d. copy and paste

_____ e. I don't know

Match the file extension to the type of document it represents:

.txt	_____ MS Excel
.doc	_____ text
.htm, .html	_____ MS Word
.jpg	_____ Acrobat Reader
.mdb	_____ MS PowerPoint
.xls	_____ MS Access
.ppt	_____ graphic
.pdf	_____ web page

A series of questions from the *Cornell Computer Skills Survey* required graduates to respond about their skill levels. An added value for these questions is the level of detail included in the statements. Graduates were queried on individual tasks in their skill set for manipulating numerical data (7 tasks), creating and managing databases (7 tasks), writing computer programs (4 tasks), preparing and producing documents (3 tasks), and using computer telecommunications networks and software (6 tasks). Graduates responded using a scale (don't know, not needed, basic skill, intermediate skill, advanced skill) that indicated the level needed for their jobs. Examples of key tasks in these areas are listed below. This question could be retooled for students enrolled in academic programs to focus on skills and tasks in word processing, information storage and retrieval, file management, mastery of presentation software, and so on.

Use a spreadsheet program such as Lotus, Excel, Quattro, or Super Cale for data entry.

Use a spreadsheet program to perform simple arithmetic calculations.

Use statistical packages, such as SPSS, SYSTAT, or SAS for statistical analyses.

Create bibliographic databases such as references to marketing articles or company reports.

Use bibliographic file management such as ProCite or NoteBook to organize downloaded citations and personal reference files.

Use a word-processing program such as WordPerfect, WriteNow, or Word to produce letters, memos, or reports.

Use a desktop publishing program such as PageMaker or Ventura to produce newsletters, brochures, or flyers.

Use electronic mail and bulletin boards to communicate with colleagues.

The following questions from the *Cal Poly–Pomona Information Competency Assessment* require short-answer responses that may provide useful data. These questions could also be appropriate for the "Students' Relationship with Faculty" section of this chapter.

How many of your classes have required you to use a computer outside of the regular class meeting time?

How many of your classes have required you to use e-mail?

How many of your classes have had web pages that included class material or required you to use the Internet?

How many of your classes have required you to use a computer to access library resources?

Researchers at Georgetown College (Kentucky) used the following questions to determine levels of technological literacy of new students. While it is unclear why the researchers asked for the importance of each of the acronyms, the initial part of the query is an excellent candidate for the short-answer format and requires students to actually demonstrate their knowledge of terms commonly used in the online environment.

> What does the acronym "FAQ" stand for and why is it important?
>
> What does the acronym "URL" stand for and why is it important?
>
> What does the acronym "HTML" stand for and why is it important?[15]

The following questions from the *Cal Poly–Pomona Information Competency Assessment* also require some level of knowledge about technology.

> Which statement about removable storage, such as Zip cartridges, is not true?
>
> a. allows you to back up your data
> b. transport files
> c. increase random access memory (RAM)
> d. increase data storage
>
> You want to make a list of the classes you plan to take next quarter showing the course number, units, days, times, instructors, and rooms. You want it to add up the number of units and be easy to format in columns. You could use any of the computer software types listed below, but what type would probably be the most straightforward?
>
> a. word processor
> b. spreadsheet
> c. database

Although the latter question is a bit wordy, it does adequately describe the situation from the student's perspective. Both of these questions would benefit from the addition of an "I don't know" option.

It is also important to ensure that the questions you ask will provide you with usable data. There is often a tendency in survey development to include questions that don't appear to be necessary or relevant in order to assess competencies. The following were taken from the *Cal Poly–Pomona Information Competency Assessment*.

> What is the typical random access memory (RAM) configuration for a computer?

a. 32MB	c. 256K
b. 2GB	d. 512 bytes

Which of the following is the best description of the Internet?

  a. A big computer somewhere that contains a large amount of information

  b. A collection of interconnected big computers managed by universities, the government, and large organizations

  c. A huge number of computers of various sizes that are connected to each other and that can belong to anyone

The second time you visit a web page in an Internet session, the page is usually faster to display on your screen than the first time. Why?

  a. Internet path already established

  b. URL compressed once you have visited a site

  c. Files that make the page are cached on your computer

  d. Really isn't faster the second time

The *Georgetown College Task-Based Technology Assessment Test* also included the following questions:

What does each part of an e-mail address represent? Which part is the "user name"? Which part is the "domain name"? Which part is the "top-domain name"? What does the @ symbol represent?

What does each part of a web address represent? Which part represents the protocol? Which part is the name of the server? Which part is the directory or folder on the server? Which part is the file being accessed? What does the / symbol represent?

Why are Internet addresses of any type (web, e-mail, etc.) always written in lowercase and always enclosed in angle brackets when included in text?

How would you describe the "To:" portion of an e-mail address? The "From:" portion? The "CC:" portion? The "BCC:" portion?

What is an "e-mail attachment"? How and when would you use an e-mail attachment? What must you do to open an e-mail attachment?

What are "computer protocols" and why are they important?

What is the difference between a "web server," a "website," a "web page," and a "home page"?

How does the citing of sources found electronically differ from sources found via traditional library research work? In other words, how would the bibliographic reference for an article or book found electronically differ from the bibliographic reference for an article or book actually on the shelf in the library? What would be the same about both references?

Librarians often recommend that faculty make sure that they themselves can complete assignments they have developed for their students. It is strongly recommended that researchers who develop and implement information literacy assessment tools do the same. The researchers at Georgetown College ask, "Why are a significant number of incoming Georgetown College students not 'technology proficient'?"[16] Although the authors do not list their own query development as a possible contributing factor, it is recommended that survey questions be as clear and unambiguous as possible in order to prevent confusion on the part of those being assessed.

NOTES

1. Teresa Y. Neely, *Sociological and Psychological Aspects of Information Literacy in Higher Education* (Lanham, MD: Scarecrow, 2002), 90.

2. Neely, *Sociological and Psychological Aspects*, 92.

3. Ibid., 147.

4. Ibid.

5. Ibid., 149. See also Arlene Greer, Lee Weston, and Mary Alm, "Assessment of Learning Outcomes: A Measure of Progress in Library Literacy," *College and Research Libraries* 52, no. 6 (1991): 549–57.

6. Heather Morrison, "Information Literacy Skills: An Exploratory Focus Group Study of Student Perceptions," *Research Strategies* 15, no. 1 (1997): 4–17.

7. Ibid.

8. Neely, *Sociological and Psychological Aspects*, 18. See also Christina S. Doyle, "Development of a Model of Information Literacy Outcome Measures within the National Education Goals of 1990" (Ph.D. diss., Northern Arizona University, 1992).

9. Neely, *Sociological and Psychological Aspects*, 137–39.

10. Clarence Toomer, "Adult Learner Perceptions of Bibliographic Instructional Services in Five Private Four-Year Liberal Arts Colleges in North Carolina" (Ed.D. diss., North Carolina State University, 1993).

11. U.S. Department of Commerce, National Telecommunications and Information Administration, "Falling through the Net: Defining the Digital Divide" (1999), http://www.ntia.doc.gov/ntiahome/fttn99/contents.html.

12. Universities of Maryland Collaborative, "Universities of Maryland Collaborative Information Literacy Grant Proposal" (working paper, 2004).

13. Universities of Maryland Collaborative, "Collaborative Information Literacy Grant Proposal."

14. For lists of technology competencies, see Old Dominion University, "Computer and Information Literacy Self-Assessment Survey," http://www.odu.edu/webroot/orgs/AO/CLT/FAssess.nsf/Computer_Information_Literacy_Survey?OpenForm; Ulla K. Bunz and Howard E. Sypher, "The Computer-Email-Web (CEW) Fluency Scale—Development and Validation," presentation at the National Communications Association Conference, Atlanta, November 1–4, 2001, ERIC ED 458 657; Ulla K. Bunz, "The Computer-Email-Web (CEW) Fluency Scale—Development and Validation," *International Journal of Human-Computer Interaction* 17, no. 4 (2004): 479–506; and William S. Rafaill and Andrea C. Peach, "Are Your Students Ready for College? Technology Literacy at Georgetown College," in Proceedings of the Annual Mid-South Instructional Technology Conference, Murfreesboro, TN, April 8–10, 2001, ERIC ED 463 728.

15. Rafaill and Peach, "Are Your Students Ready for College?"

16. Ibid.

9

Developing Information Literacy Assessment Instrumemts

Teresa Y. Neely with Jessame Ferguson

A lthough a great number of information literacy instruments have been developed for college-level students, very few of them are represented in the published literature, and even fewer are based on the ACRL Standards.

In this chapter, we will discuss how to develop a standards-based instrument to assess information literacy. We will draw on our own experience developing a survey as part of the information literacy project at the University of Maryland, Baltimore County, and we will identify and discuss types of surveys and queries that are appropriate for information literacy assessment. We will also address developing goals and objectives, research questions, and when to use various types of instruments. This chapter will also provide an analysis of individual query development and examples of query formats. This chapter should be used along with the standard chapters (3 through 7) and chapter 8 to assist you in developing an information literacy instrument that is appropriate for your needs.

Developing an information literacy instrument first requires some groundwork, including gaining the support of administrators and others in the organization, assessing other instruments that are available, and creating goals and objectives that will help drive the process. In this chapter, we will cover these areas as well as provide guidance on how to write the survey questions themselves.

THE FIRST STEP: GARNER INSTITUTIONAL SUPPORT

Successful survey instruments cannot be developed in a vacuum. It is important to obtain input and feedback from the teaching faculty, students, library faculty and staff, and university administration. In fact, a key ACRL best practice for information literacy programs is administrative and institutional support.[1]

Perhaps the most important place to begin eliciting support is at the top. The support of the head of the library can be instrumental to the success of an information literacy program in a variety of ways. A library director can use his or her influence and position on campus to further the cause of the information literacy program as a whole and to lobby support for institutional assessment. The library director can provide entrée to the provost's council or other top-level university bodies, and to the faculty senate or its equivalent, and he or she can assist the head of reference or the information literacy coordinator in gaining an audience with various groups and department heads on campus.

By contrast, if your library director does not support information literacy instruction, you will be fighting an uphill battle in developing an information literacy program and championing the need for assessment. It is therefore important to keep the head of the library informed and involved throughout the assessment process.

At the University of Maryland, Baltimore County, the library director played a key role in gaining the support of the Provost's Council for the assessment project. By attending a Provost's Council meeting with the head of reference, who explained the project and assessment and provided a one-page handout, the members of the council were able to ask questions and provide input into the project from the very beginning. The chief information officer for the university's Office of Information Technology was also present, and it was his suggestion that the instrument be deployed using the university's information portal, my.UMBC.edu. Similar audiences were gained with the chairs of departments with a history of being active with the library. These departments were the primary targets when considering a student population for information literacy assessment at the University of Maryland, Baltimore County, in the fall of 2003.

In some cases, it may be relatively easy to gain the support of administrators. For example, if students have confessed to cheating or if other information-related infractions have occurred, campus administrators would likely welcome the data the assessment provides so they can develop policies and procedures for addressing these problems.

In addition, accreditation agencies are now including information literacy in their requirements for accreditation. The Middle States Commission on Higher Education was the first accrediting agency to include information literacy criteria, based on the ACRL Standards, in its accreditation process; and at least five other accrediting agencies have followed suit, recognizing the importance of information literacy in the higher education process.[2]

In terms of the organizational structure of your library's reference and public services departments, you may want to consider reorganizing to better support instruction and information literacy efforts. With the support of your library director and the public services and reference department heads, it may be possible to reorganize the reference department to create an instruction group or team that would be responsible for conceiving, developing, implementing, and evaluating an information literacy program, including assessment.

WHY ARE YOU ASSESSING?

Before developing an assessment instrument, you must first determine why you are conducting the research. What is the purpose of the survey? The answer to that question will guide you through the development process.

For example, a short information literacy pre- and posttest to address short-term skills deficiencies or to determine current skill sets may be sufficient when you are assessing the following:

> Students' acquisition of individual skills; e.g., developing a thesis statement or search strategies
>
> Students' knowledge of local resources and facilities; e.g., what is the name of the library's online catalog? Where is the reference department located?
>
> Subject-specific knowledge for a particular course; e.g., what does *ERIC* stand for? Where would you go to find scholarly information on child abuse and domestic violence?
>
> Other information you may want to know; e.g., attitudes about or knowledge of librarians

As a rule of thumb, pre- and posttests should not be identical, though they may be similar. Posttest results may be biased if students memorize the correct response. If tests must be identical, queries should be renumbered at the very least.

On other occasions, a pre- or posttest would not be suitable. If, for example, the purpose of the assessment is to determine baseline knowledge for a large number of students representing a diversity of majors—either once or over a period of time (longitudinally)—then a more comprehensive and generalized instrument is in order. The goal of these types of surveys is to assess students' general standards and skills while de-emphasizing their knowledge of subject-specific and localized resources.

The important point is to think through your purpose before developing the assessment instrument. The goals and objectives of the assessment— along with any research questions and hypotheses—should be directly connected to and, ideally, developed prior to the development of the actual survey queries. It is far better to have the questions in mind before developing the survey than to try and use survey data to answer research questions developed after the survey has been completed.

In the case of the UMBC's information literacy program, the following goals and objectives were developed for assessment purposes:

> To gather baseline data on the information literacy skills of UMBC students
>
> To use the data gathered to assist in the development of an information literacy program for students, faculty, and staff at UMBC

Although there were only two goals, they were interconnected and were critically important to the future of the overall UMBC instruction program: the data gathered to determine baseline levels of information literacy skills were used to develop an information literacy program for the campus.

Other goals and objectives for assessment may focus on individual standards, performance indicators, and objectives, such as the following:

> To gather data on the information literacy skills of students enrolled in a particular course, at a particular academic level (undergraduate, graduate), etc.
>
> To determine whether college-level students know when to recognize a need for information
>
> To determine whether college-level students know how to access information effectively and efficiently

To determine whether college-level students know how to evaluate information and its sources critically

To determine whether college-level students know how to incorporate selected information into their knowledge base and value system

To determine whether college-level students know how to use information effectively to accomplish a specific purpose

To determine whether college-level students understand many of the economic, legal, and social issues surrounding the use of information

To determine whether college-level students use information ethically and legally

Once you have developed specific goals and objectives for your survey, the next step is to develop specific research questions and hypotheses. What theories and assumptions do you have about your population? What do you know about possible results? What do you want to know, prove, or disprove? Based on anecdotal evidence available in every library—primarily consisting of reference desk encounters, bibliographic instruction interactions, and the inevitable one-shot lectures—you should be able to determine what you know about the possible research results, what the important issues are, and what information would help you support or disprove your hypotheses.

The following research questions were developed by the UMBC Task Force to address the perceived deficiencies and needs of students at the university. These can also be used as a starting point when developing your own research questions and hypotheses.

What are the attitudes of college-level students about Christina S. Doyle's information literacy skills?[3]

To what extent do [UMBC] students tend to overestimate their information-literacy confidence levels?

To what extent are [UMBC] students unable to identify the basic elements of a bibliographic citation?

To what extent are [UMBC] students aware of what constitutes plagiarism?

To what extent are [UMBC] students familiar with the concept of fair use?

To what extent are [UMBC] students familiar with the concept of copyright?

Do [UMBC] students who self-report a high level of confidence with information literacy skills perform well when responding to questions that represent those skills?

Do [UMBC] students who self-report a high level of confidence with computers perform well when responding to questions that represent information literacy skills?

To what extent do [UMBC] faculty model good library use behavior?

To what extent do [UMBC] faculty encourage students to use the library?

REVIEW OF EXISTING INSTRUMENTS

Before developing an information literacy assessment instrument, it is a good idea to review the literature to see what others have done. This will prevent you from reinventing the wheel and will also allow you to benefit from the work of others. The UMBC Task Force has done much of the work for you in this regard. However, if you wish to update the list of survey instruments compiled for this book (see the appendix), keep in mind that there has been little research in information literacy, and much of what is available has been done as a part of dissertations and master's theses. In addition to identifying instruments via the research literature, we strongly recommend that you search the World Wide Web.

In the process of developing our instrument, the UMBC Task Force identified and reviewed more than seventy information literacy survey instruments to determine whether they were based on the ACRL Standards or on elements of the standards. We found that most of the information literacy instruments for assessing college-level students were posted on the Web and were not published in the literature. One benefit of using the Web to facilitate and promote information literacy instruction and assessment is that it is unmediated. It is limited only to the guidelines of the Internet service provider or the home institution. Thus, information literacy surveys can be posted indefinitely for an infinite audience. However, there are pitfalls to using this medium as well. We found several breaches of good web etiquette and authoring in the surveys we reviewed. Many were not dated, were out of date, or did not have contact information. If you decide to post survey instruments on the Web, remember to include identifying information (including dates) on all web pages, word-processed documents, and PDF (Portable Document Format) documents in order to ensure appropriate credit and recognition for your hard work.

We were able to characterize the instruments we reviewed into the following categories, based on their purpose:

> To test students' knowledge, attitudes, or competencies with the local library web page, online catalog, or other locally owned or subscription resources (databases)
>
> To test students' knowledge of resources in a particular subject, major, or academic discipline
>
> To gather attitudinal or self-report data from students
>
> To determine students' technological competencies
>
> To gather data on incoming freshmen's skills
>
> To compare pre- and posttest results for short-term intervention purposes

Many of the instruments we reviewed contained similar or identical queries, making it difficult to determine which instrument originated the query. Few of the instruments identified were designed with the ACRL Standards in mind, which is understandable given that the standards were approved in January 2000 and published in March of that same year. Still, many of the instruments contained elements of the standards, which reflects how reference and instruction librarians have long been concerned about students' ability to identify appropriate resources for their information needs, develop successful search strategies, evaluate information, and employ critical thinking skills.

The *UMBC Survey* is one of the few instruments currently available that was developed solely with the ACRL Standards in mind. A group of researchers at Kent State University (Ohio) are developing a survey based on the standards, but their approach is a little different. The purpose of Kent State University's project for the Standardized Assessment of Information Literacy Skills (SAILS) "is to develop an instrument for programmatic-level assessment of information literacy skills." The researchers are using a systems approach to develop queries and "an item response theory for data analysis" to develop an instrument that can be used across institutions. Once the instrument is validated, it will be used to assess the skills of incoming college-level students and to determine long-term improvements or other changes in students' skill levels over time.[4]

Other survey instruments based on the ACRL Standards include the Portland State University Library's *Information Literacy Inventory*, the *Bay Area Community Colleges Assessment Project*, and a dissertation based solely on Standard 2.

The Portland instrument, though not completed or updated since July 2001, is clearly divided into sections based on the ACRL Standards. The purpose of the *Bay Area Community Colleges Assessment Project* was to "develop and field test an information competency exam for California Community College students." The exam was developed based on the ACRL outcomes from standards 1, 2, 3, and 5.[5] Connie E. Constantino's 2003 dissertation included a "questionnaire and interview" addressing Standard 2.[6] In addition, the Minneapolis Community and Technical College has developed information literacy midterm and final exams for its Information Literacy and Research Skills course, INFS 1000, that satisfy the college's information literacy requirement. These exams are mapped to the ACRL objectives.[7] None of the other seventy instruments we reviewed specifically mentioned or referred to the standards.

In November 2004 the Educational Testing Service (ETS) announced a partnership with seven colleges and universities to develop the Information and Communication Technology (ICT) Literacy Assessment, which will build on the ACRL Standards, among others.[8] The project defines *information and communication technology literacy* as

> the ability to use digital technology, communications tools and/or networks appropriately to solve information problems in order to function in an information society. This includes the ability to use technology as a tool to research, organize, evaluate and communicate information, and the possession of a fundamental understanding of the ethical/legal issues surrounding the access and use of information.[9]

The ICT Literacy Assessment is different from most information literacy and library research assessment tools in that it is "simulation-based," assessing multiple aspects of ICT competencies by "requiring test takers to use basic technology as a tool to arrive at solutions," instead of posing multiple-choice queries. Examples of some of the sixteen tasks that students tackle in a two-hour session include building a spreadsheet and composing e-mail messages that summarize research findings.[10]

On March 3, 2005, the ETS announced that by the end of that month, approximately 8,000 students nationwide would have taken the assessment. Aggregate results will only be released to participating institutions during the first year or so of launching. Although an ETS presentation at the American Library Association's Annual Conference in June 2005 reported that students involved in beta testing of the assessment gave overall positive feedback, responses from the library community were less encouraging, noting there was "not enough emphasis on print media" and "too much emphasis on technology" in the assessment.[11]

DEVELOPING SURVEY INSTRUMENTS

As mentioned previously, surveys for information literacy can be characterized in a number of ways. For the purposes of this book, we will focus on the development of a generalized survey, based on the ACRL Standards, to assess baseline information literacy levels and competencies for college-level students.

The benefit of developing a survey that is more standard-specific than subject- or institution-based is that students will be tested on broad concepts and skills rather than on localized information. It is important to teach students that there is a world of resources beyond the institution's online catalog and that databases owned by the local library do not necessarily represent all of the resources that are potentially available. Students who learn only about the resources owned by a particular library are often unable to make the transition to using similar resources in other libraries. Key subject-specific resources should be introduced and reinforced in the classroom. Ideally, students should be exposed to and become familiar with key print and online resources, including the identification and review of key journals and other professional literature in the field by their faculty.

When developing an ACRL Standards–based survey, do not be daunted by the number of performance indicators and outcomes listed in the standards. There are more than 100 outcomes that fall under the five standards. You certainly do not need to include all performance indicators or outcomes in every assessment effort. Just include the ones that are relevant for the needs of your institution. Chapters 3 through 7 provide in-depth discussions that address the writing of queries for each of the standards. These chapters also include examples of queries and identify and discuss the types of queries that are most applicable for assessing that standard.

Also, keep in mind that query development is an ongoing process. Once you have developed an instrument, be prepared to add, delete, update, and revise queries on a regular basis. Query development requires a great deal of hard work, and one instrument will never be *the* answer to all of your assessment dilemmas. Many aspects should be considered in information literacy assessment, and it is virtually impossible to develop an instrument that will address them all adequately. Be realistic and recognize that surveying students is only one aspect of assessment. Try investigating other qualitative methods of assessing students along with a survey, such as behavioral observations, portfolios of student work (including papers and assignments), and research diaries.

HOW TO WRITE A QUERY

Types of Queries

All queries are not created equal. Typically, information literacy assessment uses various categories and formats of queries.

True/false or yes/no queries (e.g., "Have you ever had formal library instruction?"). Depending on the query, these types may require a follow-up or related query to ensure the collection of usable data. For example, using a true/false or yes/no query would be appropriate in the following query:

Do you use e-mail?

Yes   No   Don't know

However, the following query would not provide enough usable data due to the lack of specificity:

Do you use productivity software?

Yes   No   Don't know

This response does not tell you what kind of productivity software the student has used or if the student even knows what productivity software is. This query, from the *CSU Minimum Competency Survey*, could be rewritten to add the following in parentheses after the question: Microsoft Word, Excel, Access, PowerPoint. Alternatively, a follow-up question could be written:

If yes, which ones?

____ Microsoft Word ____ Excel ____ Access ____ PowerPoint

If the objective of this query is to find out the extent of students' experience with the software, additional queries would need to be written eliciting information on students' comfort levels with and knowledge of software functionality. For example, students could be given a list of descriptions (e.g., "Which software would you use to compile a database for your CD collection?") and asked to match the description to the software. Or the queries could be written in a multiple-choice format, including four different queries describing examples of uses of software, with the same pull-down menu containing the four types of software.

Multiple-choice queries (e.g., "The best place to look for an introduction to a topic such as astronomy is: a, b, c, d"). This type of query requires the respondent to select one or more options. This query should always include an "I don't know" option to discourage guessing.

Matching queries (e.g., "Match the file extension to the type of document it represents"). This type of query works similar to the pull-down menu.

Short-answer queries (e.g., "What do we call a book written by an individual about her or his own life?") and *essay-type queries* (e.g., "What might be a research question to investigate 'whether governments should get involved in regulating the use of the Internet'?") work best in short- term pre- and posttest assessments. These queries are also ideal for use with smaller populations.

Attitudinal/self-report queries (e.g., "strongly agree, agree, undecided, disagree, strongly disagree"; or "very comfortable, comfortable, undecided/ neutral, uncomfortable, very uncomfortable"). These queries use Likert-type scales and generally require additional follow-up or related queries in order to provide a more holistic picture of students' actual abilities.

Demographic queries (e.g., age, academic status). These queries can be written in a variety of ways. The most common formats are multiple choice (e.g., select age from a range); pull-down menu (e.g., select race, major, or academic status from a predefined list); and short answer/fill in the blank.

Some types of queries are better suited for automated test environments than others. Make sure that you are writing queries that work well in an automated environment. Multiple-choice, pull-down menus, true/false, yes/no, matching, and Likert-scale multiple-choice queries work well in an automated environment.

The use of short-answer or essay-type questions requires text fields, and while these types allow for more flexibility and creativity on the part of the respondent, they may prove to be problematic in working with and analyzing results. Figure 10-3 (in chapter 10) demonstrates the complexity in reporting text box fields from the *UMBC Survey* query: "Which Internet search engine do you use?" The majority of the responses were for Google, but actual responses typed in included google, google.com, and www.google.com. Each of these responses required a separate field to report responses. This problem is eliminated when the query requires a standardized response, such as in a multiple-choice or pull-down menu query format.

It is generally a good idea to include an "I don't know" option in each query, including those that require a yes/no or true/false response. This provides the student with a valid option for selection.

Do's and Dont's of Writing Queries

In developing individual queries, there are certain things you need to consider. This section uses examples from the instruments we reviewed to provide some guidance for writing your own queries.

All queries should be adapted or written from the perspective of college-level students. Use language such as, "If you were developing your own personal web page," "What would you do if," or "If you were giving a presentation on," so that the student has a context for responding to the query and is not confused about what you are asking. The following question was taken from the *UMBC Survey*.

> *Example:* If you were creating your own website, which of the following could you legally use on your web page without permission?
>
> a. Pictures of Britney Spears from the Internet
>
> b. The theme song from *Titanic* by Celine Dion
>
> c. Letters that you found at the National Archives written by Martha to her husband, President George Washington
>
> d. President George W. Bush's Inaugural Speech
>
> e. Pictures of Anna Kournikova you scanned in from *Sports Illustrated* magazine

    f. Text you scanned in from *Harry Potter and the Prisoner of Azkaban*

    g. Text of the Homeland Security Act introduced in Congress

    h. Text of an article from *Newsweek* criticizing the Homeland Security Act that you scanned in

Note that this query uses popular culture and relevant national issues to sound current and to maintain the interest of college-level students. The use of citations on hip-hop, file sharing, sports, music, and movies may be more appropriate and interesting to college-level students than the Cuban Missile Crisis or the Savings and Loan Scandal. At the very least, students should be reasonably familiar with the examples you use to illustrate concepts. This approach is used successfully by many bibliographic instruction librarians during sessions with students to connect and maintain their interest. The following question was also taken from the *UMBC Survey*.

Decide whether each citation below refers to a

    a. book

    b. book chapter

    c. journal article

    d. newspaper article

    e. conference proceedings

    f. government document

    g. thesis or dissertation

    h. not sure

    ____ Rosen, Ralph M., and Donald R. Marks. "Comedies of transgression in gangsta rap and ancient classical poetry." New Literary History 30 (1999): 897–929.

    ____ Keeling, Kara. "'A homegrown revolutionary'?: Tupac Shakur and the legacy of the Black Panther Party." Black Scholar 29 (1999): 59–64.

    ____ Rhoden, William C. "After a Trying Year, Ray Lewis Triumphs." New York Times, 8 Jan. 2001, D3.

    ____ United States Congress. Commission on Security and Cooperation in Europe. Deterioration of freedom of the media in OSCA countries: hearing before the commission on Security and cooperation in Europe. 106th Cong., 1st sess. Washington: GPO, 2000.

_____ Woodfork, Joshua Carter. "(Dis)claiming whiteness: Homer Plessy, Tiger Woods, and racially transformed parents." Master's thesis. Michigan State University, 1999.

_____ Fox, Thomas C. Sexuality and Catholicism. New York: G. Braziller, 2000.

_____ Rushkoff, Douglas. "Ecstasy: Prescription for cultural renaissance. In Ecstasy: The complete guide: A comprehensive look at the risks and benefits of MDMA, edited by Julie Holland, 350–357. Rochester, VT: Park Street Press, 2001.

_____ Freed, Barbara F., ed. Foreign language acquisition research and the classroom. Proc. of Consortium for Language, Teaching and Learning Conference, Oct., 1989, U of Pennsylvania. Lexington: Heath, 1991.

Write queries that require students to demonstrate their attitudes toward, knowledge of, or abilities with a particular standard, performance indicator, or outcome. For example, if you ask students how they feel about "developing successful search strategies," be sure to include related queries that require them to identify, define, or respond to examples of search strategies. The combined responses will provide you with a more holistic picture of the abilities of your population.

Write queries aimed at your primary audience. Do not use jargon or acronyms without explaining or defining them.

> When conducting research in electronic databases, how often do you use the following searching techniques? [very frequently, frequently, occasionally, infrequently, never]
>
> > Truncation (search using * or $ as the last letter(s) of word, e.g., child*)
> >
> > Boolean operator "AND" (e.g., rivers AND pollution)
> >
> > Boolean operator "OR" (e.g., Blacks OR African Americans)
> >
> > Boolean operator "NOT" (e.g., dolphins NOT football)
> >
> > Limiters (limit search by date, publisher, language, type of material)

Proximity operators "NEAR," "BETWEEN" (e.g., housing NEAR development)

Cross- and multiple-field searching (Search more than one field at a time, such as publisher, journal title, author, descriptors, etc.)

Use LCSH, *ERIC* descriptors or some other controlled vocabulary[12]

If students do not recognize or understand what you mean by *truncation, Boolean,* or *proximity operators,* then they will not be able to answer the query correctly and your results will be biased. Claudia J. Morner's instrument, the *Morner Test,* includes a question that defines the term *truncation* without compromising the survey question itself:

Truncation is a library computer-searching term meaning that the last letter or letters of a word are substituted with a symbol, such as "*" or "$". A good reason you might truncate a search term such as child* is that truncation will

a. limit search to descriptor or subject heading field

b. reduce the number of irrelevant citations

c. save searcher typing time

d. yield more citations

e. I don't know

It is commonly known in academic libraries that *primary source* does not mean the same thing to a history professor as it does to a theater professor or one in the sciences. Librarians, curators, and archivists also use varying definitions of this term. The following type of query, from the *UCLA Library Instructional Services Advisory Committee Questionnaire,* is most effective when a commonly agreed-upon definition has been established.

For your history class, you must select a primary source and write a brief paper placing it in context. From the list below, choose the one best primary source on which to base your paper.

a. chapter in your textbook

b. journal article

c. scholarly monograph

d. collection of letters

e. critical biography

f. don't know

If you must assess students' knowledge of databases and other resources, define the scope and nature of the resource in the context of the query. The following query from Wartburg College's *Information Literacy Pre-Test for IS 201* illustrates this point.

> Which database would be best for finding information for a two-page paper about violence in schools?
>
> a. *Primary Search.* Provides full text for 57 children's magazines and over 100 children's pamphlets, designed for the elementary school student.
>
> b. *Newspaper Source.* Contains full text for regional U.S. newspapers, international newspapers, newswires, and newspaper columns, as well as other sources. This database also contains indexing and abstracts for national newspapers.
>
> c. *Academic Search Premier.* Provides full text for more than 3,460 scholarly publications covering academic areas of study, including social sciences, humanities, education, computer sciences, engineering, language and linguistics, arts and literature, medical sciences, and ethnic studies. This database is updated on a daily basis.
>
> d. *WorldCat.* OCLC catalog of books, web resources, and other material worldwide. Contains all the records cataloged by OCLC member libraries. Offers millions of bibliographic records. Includes records representing 400 languages. Over 41,000,000 records.

Avoid confusing queries. Including similarly spelled or pronounced words in a multiple-choice question may confuse students and motivate them to guess, thereby influencing incorrect responses.

> A bibliography is
>
> a. a book about a person
>
> b. a collection of maps and charts
>
> c. a list of references
>
> d. a directory of names

> The term used to describe a list of books, articles, web pages, and other materials that might have some relationship to each other is
>
> a. an autobiography

  b. a bibliography

  c. a biography

  d. a footnote

The first query above (culled from a variety of survey instruments reviewed) and the second one (taken from Anne Cooper Moore's 2001 dissertation) could be confusing to students because the words *bibliography* and *biography* could potentially be confused.

  What is Boolean Logic?

    a. New Math

    b. Search Operators

    c. Eastern Philosophy

    d. None of the Above

    e. I Don't Know

    f. All of the Above

This query, from Lana Webb Jackman's 1999 dissertation, could be confusing because all of the responses are capitalized, possibly indicating they are all formal titles or proper names. Additionally, none of these responses can be grouped as similar responses except d, e, and f.

  Articles from which one of the following periodicals are consistently appropriate for use in a research paper?

    a. *Science*

    b. *Redbook*

    c. *Atlantic Monthly*

    d. *Newsweek*

    e. *Psychology Today*

In analyzing this latter query, also from Moore's dissertation, most college-level students could eliminate *Redbook* and *Newsweek*, and many could further eliminate *Atlantic Monthly*, but how is a college-level student to differentiate between the remaining two publications? Does *Science* have the edge over *Psychology Today*? It is preferable to use examples that are clear indications of the periodical type and are familiar to students.

  Not giving proper acknowledgement for another writer's work, thought, or argument is known as:

a. originalism

b. citation

c. referencing

d. plagiarism

It is acceptable and encouraged to use humor in queries, but making up new words or using esoteric and possibly unfamiliar terminology, such as response a in this query from the *Maryville Inventory*, may have a negative effect and cause confusion.

Placement of Queries

Once you have written, developed, or adapted all your queries, it is time to assemble your survey instrument. The following are general tips to be considered when assembling your instrument:

> The first question is often the most important one on a survey. It should be connected clearly to the survey's purpose.
>
> Put objective questions before subjective ones so that respondents feel comfortable.
>
> Move from the most familiar to the least familiar questions.
>
> Follow a natural time sequence.
>
> Put relatively easy questions at the end. This is particularly important in long surveys.
>
> Put demographic questions at the end. They're considered sensitive, so if they are at the end of a survey, respondents have time to "warm up" to answering them.[13]

For additional tips on query development in general, consult the articles "How to Design Online Surveys" by Susanne E. Gaddis and "Writing Test Questions like a Pro" by Greg Conderman and Carol Koroghlanian.[14]

NOTES

1. Association of College and Research Libraries, "Characteristics of Programs of Information Literacy That Illustrate Best Practices," *College and Research Libraries News* 64, no. 1 (January 2003): 32–35.

2. The other five accrediting agencies are the Western Association of Schools and Colleges, Southern Association of Colleges and Schools, Northwest Association of Schools

and Colleges, North Central Association of Colleges and Schools, and the New England Association of Schools and Colleges.

3. Christina S. Doyle, "Development of a Model of Information Literacy Outcome Measures within National Education Goals of 1990" (Ph.D. diss., Northern Arizona University, 1992), 2.

4. Lisa G. O'Connor, Carolyn J. Radcliff, and Julie A. Gedeon, "Applying Systems Design and Item Response Theory to the Problem of Measuring Information Literacy Skills," *College and Research Libraries* 63, no. 6 (November 2002): 528–43. See also http://www.projectsails.org.

5. Bay Area Community Colleges Assessment Project Team, *Bay Area Community Colleges Assessment Project: A Two-Part Information Competency Assessment Exam,* http://www.topsy.org/ICAP/ICAProject.html. The Bay Area Community Colleges Assessment Project Team includes Bonnie Gratch-Lindauer, project leader, Pam Baker, Amelie Brown, Micca Gray, Andy Kivel, Brian Lym, and Topsy Smalley.

6. Connie E. Constantino, "Stakeholders' Perceptions of the Importance of Information Literacy Competencies within Undergraduate Education," (Ed.D. diss., Alliant International University, 2003).

7. Minneapolis Community and Technical College, "Information Literacy and Research Skills—INFS 1000," http://db.mctc.mnscu.edu/library/courses/infs1000/infs1000.htm.

8. Educational Testing Service, "ETS Launches ICT Literacy Assessment, an Online Measure of Student Information and Communication Technology Proficiency" (November 8, 2004), http://www.ets.org/ictliteracy/educator.html. Along with ETS, the seven charter colleges and universities make up the National Higher Education ICT Initiative are the California Community College System; California State University System; University of California, Los Angeles; University of Louisville; University of North Alabama; University of Texas System; and the University of Washington.

9. Educational Testing Service, *ICT Literacy Assessment: Do Your Students Have the ICT Skills They Need to Succeed?* (brochure, 2005).

10. Educational Testing Service, "ETS Launches ICT Literacy Assessment."

11. Educational Testing Service, "ETS ICT Literacy Assessment Premieres at Portland State University: New Test Measures Students' Ability to Process and Communicate Information in a Technological Environment" (March 3, 2005), http://www.ets.org/ictliteacy/05030901.html; Ilene Rockman, Gordon Smith, and Irvin R. Katz, "An Overview of the Higher Education ICT Literacy Assessment," presentation at the American Library Association's Annual Conference, Chicago, June 23–29, 2005.

12. "LCSH" and "ERIC" are spelled out in the *UMBC Survey*.

13. Susanne E. Gaddis, "How to Design Online Surveys," *Training and Development* 15, no. 6 (June 1998): 67–71.

14. Gaddis, "How to Design Online Surveys"; Greg Conderman and Carol Koroghlanian, "Writing Test Questions like a Pro," *Intervention in School and Clinic* 38, no. 2 (November 2002): 83–87.

Automating Assessment Instruments

Jay J. Patel and Teresa Y. Neely with Jessame Ferguson

A utomating a survey instrument involves a wide range of issues, from staffing to compatibility with the campus system. In this chapter, we will discuss these issues in the context of the automation of the *UMBC Survey*. We will discuss how to select staff with appropriate skills for instrument automation and will also include a glossary of relevant technical terminology. We will address technology compatibility with local area network platforms, as well as campus network platforms; the selection and use of an operating system, web server software, and web programming language; automated instrument aesthetics; query design issues; and testing. Database development, data analysis, and data reports will also be discussed.

STAFFING

Once the UMBC Task Force decided that an automated survey instrument would be the most appropriate method for assessing incoming students, we immediately recognized that no one on the task force possessed the technical skills necessary to do the automation or build an accompanying database. We decided to look outside the task force for assistance.

The graduate school of the University of Maryland, Baltimore County, provides funding opportunities for graduate students to work throughout the campus. Campus departments submit a job description and students apply for specific jobs. The graduate school distributes completed applications to participating departments, and if selected, students are paid through the graduate school. When we wanted to hire someone to automate the UMBC's assessment instrument, we found a graduate student funded through this program.

Students, both graduate and undergraduate, should not be overlooked as a source for the technological expertise needed to pursue your information literacy program and agenda. In fact, an undergraduate student (double) majoring in theater and computer science was responsible for the animation and programming of the Data Game at Colorado State University,[1] and an undergraduate student majoring in computer science was responsible for automating the instrument and building the accompanying database for Neely's 2000 dissertation.[2]

In selecting staff for instrument automation, it is important to look for a skill set that combines good web programming skills with sufficient knowledge of relational databases. The staff member should also possess excellent interpersonal and communications skills in order to interact with library faculty, staff, and others from various campus departments. The UMBC Task Force hired a graduate student in computer science to automate the instrument and participate as a task force member. In this position, he interacted on a regular basis not only with the task force and reference department but also with campus employees from the Office of Information Technology (including the chief information officer), the director of the library, library faculty, instruction librarians from other University System of Maryland campuses, and the director of the Office of Faculty Development at UMBC.

The following job description was designed specifically for the position:

> The Student Library Associate will assist reference librarians by providing support and technical expertise to various reference projects, including developing the technical aspect of Web-based user interfaces, tutorials, and stand alone modules for information literacy—content will be developed by librarians; designing and developing various reference-related databases (statistics, survey data, etc.); and reviewing, updating, and maintaining Web pages for reference, instruction, and other areas as needed. Associates can expect to be hired based on their skill set relating to an individual reference project.

The Associate should have a basic understanding of how information is organized, relational database development, technical competence with computers and databases, word processing, HTML, and production software. The associate should also be motivated, able to work in a team-based collaborative environment or independently, possess excellent oral and written communication skills, display demonstrated professionalism, and good judgment skills, and have excellent interpersonal skills.

When writing job descriptions, it is important to ask for what you need. Once you know what types of skills you require for instrument automation, it is critical to put those in the job description. If you are unsure of the exact skills needed, talk to the head of library computing services or the equivalent in your library. Personnel from this department may also be willing to assist you when interviewing for this position.

This particular job description elicited responses from potential candidates with technical backgrounds as well as those with graphic design backgrounds. While you might be tempted to hire someone with the graphic design background to ensure that the website or instrument will be aesthetically pleasing, you must make your decision based on functionality and the technological needs of your particular program. The job description posted by the UMBC Task Force covers a lot of ground, including the development of web-based interfaces for a variety of projects (tutorials, modules), database development (specifically relational), and web page development. Of specific concern for the *UMBC Survey*, the task force decided that they needed someone who had a basic understanding of how information is organized—a basic tenet of working in libraries. The task force also wanted someone who had great interpersonal and communication skills and the ability to work alone, as well as in a team environment.

Once the job description is finalized and the applicant selected, it is important to treat the new hire as an integral part of the group. At the University of Maryland, Baltimore County, the graduate student assistant (GSA) operated as a full member of the task force. He attended regularly scheduled meetings and provided feedback and input during instrument development. This is important. Instrument automation should not be isolated from the development process, and the person responsible for automating the instrument should know the overall goals and objectives for instrumentation. By attending meetings, the GSA had the opportunity to understand the kind of data being collected and why, which helped him develop a database that would support the goals and objectives of the assessment. Similarly, the task force, as the developers of the instrument, needed to know about the possibilities and limitations of the web-based medium they had chosen for instrument development and implementation. For example, if designed improperly, test takers' use of the back button of a web browser may cause a set of responses to be submitted multiple times. Keeping the GSA in the loop ensures that the transition from a paper-based instrument to a web-based one is smooth.

HARDWARE AND SOFTWARE COMPATIBILITY ISSUES

If you are supervising a project such as this, it is important to have some familiarity with the technology used in order to make decisions about the operating system platform, software compatibility, and integration with the campus system. To ensure compatibility with the existing local area network system, the campus's office of information technology or its equivalent must be aware of and involved in the project to automate the instrument. Their input and cooperation is often essential for the successful integration of the instrument within the campus computing environment.

There is typically a choice between two major operating system platforms: Microsoft Windows–based or Unix/Linux-based. It is important to be aware of the operating system used on the web server where you are planning to host the instrument. Knowing and understanding the operating system platform is essential in deciding which software you use to develop your database, and also which web programming language you choose. Examples of widely used web server software are the Apache web server and Microsoft Internet Information Service (IIS).

The choice of the web programming language depends to a certain degree on the operating system platform and the web server software. HTML (Hypertext Markup Language) can be used to display the text of the instrument, but storing the responses will require a more advanced web programming language. If you choose to use a Microsoft Windows–based system with IIS as your web server software, then using Active Server Pages may make the most sense. If, on the other hand, you are going to use a Unix/Linux-based system using Apache web server software, then you can use CGI/Perl as the web-based programming language. Apache web server software is open source software and is available for both Microsoft Windows NT and Unix/Linux platforms. PHP (PHP: Hypertext Preprocessor) provides a certain degree of platform independence and can be installed on most of the available web server platforms.

Irrespective of the web programming language used, the survey will most likely require the use of JavaScripting. JavaScript is widely used on web pages for form validation and verification of user responses. It was developed by Netscape and is supported by all major browsers, including Internet Explorer and Netscape. This language is embedded directly into HTML and is used for adding interactivity on web pages.

QUERY CUSTOMIZATION

The wording and expected responses to survey queries figure considerably into the automation of those survey items. The survey instrument can be automated in such a way that when the "None of the above" option is selected, all of the other options will be disabled. Designing the instrument in this way will prevent the user from causing erroneous data to be submitted for analysis. When the student checks the "All of the above" option, all of the other responses to a particular query need to be checked as well. Failure to design this into the automated query will result in faulty data. Another important thing to consider is whether you want all the questions to be compulsory. In other words, should you force survey participants to respond to all queries, prohibiting them from advancing to the next page of the survey unless they respond to all of the items? In higher education, for the most part, you cannot require research participants to take a survey; you can only hope that you get a significant response rate. In that same vein, once you have willing participants, you do not want to alienate or frustrate them by including barriers to survey completion. However, on the off chance that a participant inadvertently skips a query and proceeds to the next page, it would be a good idea to have a window appear that prompts users to respond to skipped queries.

DATABASE DEVELOPMENT

Generally, your institution will have a database system already in use, and it would be best to use what is already available and supported on campus. However, if you have a choice, there are additional compatibility issues to consider when selecting the appropriate database. Database selection also depends upon operating system platforms. If the operating system of choice is Microsoft Windows NT, then using Microsoft Access or MS SQL Server may make the most sense. Oracle, MySQL, and DB2 also provide robust alternatives. On a Unix/Linux platform, Oracle is often the preferred choice. Another factor to consider is the size of the database. Most of the databases mentioned above can easily handle more than 10,000 table rows, with each row representing a completed survey. To get optimal performance when storing, managing, and analyzing large amounts of data, it is widely accepted that Oracle is the best choice.

When developing a relational database, each table should have a primary key. This is a unique identifier for each row of the database table. It is usually the first column of the table. The value for this field can be anything from a unique user name to unique numbers. The primary benefit of having a unique identifier is that you can track the responses of a particular student throughout the survey. To keep the responses anonymous, it is suggested that a unique number be used instead of a unique user name.

It is advisable to convert text responses to numerical responses if any statistical analysis needs to be performed. If queries are developed using a Likert scale, then corresponding values submitted to the database should be on a scale from 5 to 1, or 1 to 5, or any unique numbers used consistently.

INSTRUMENT AESTHETICS

Once the compatibility issues have been resolved, the next step is to decide how you want the instrument to appear visually. Issues like the color, font size, and screen area resolution should be carefully considered. The ideal font size for most text is 12 point. Web page headings may use a larger font size. Using a smaller font size is not advisable, as it would make the text difficult to read. Text position and table spacing should be tested on multiple monitor sizes with different browsers to assure readability for students with a variety of equipment. It is also important to select web page colors with accessibility issues for the visually impaired in mind. You should be aware of issues such as the following ones:

> Most people diagnosed with color blindness have trouble distinguishing between green and red. For some people green objects appear yellow, as red and green make yellow. So if a site

contains green text on a yellow background or vice versa, then both the text and background appear yellow, making the text invisible.

Black and white are the best options for text and background, respectively. It is a good idea to design the site in black and white first; once you are satisfied with the layout, begin to add color.

Distinguishing hyperlinks by color only is not recommended. Using both a color and an underline is more effective.[3]

Once the accessibility issues are worked out, you might want to consider ways to make the survey instrument and accompanying website more appealing visually. For the UMBC Task Force's purposes, a reference student employee who was a graphic art major worked with the GSA to develop a design that was visually appealing as well as compliant with the Americans with Disabilities Act. It is important to use all of the resources at your disposal. The task force was able to use the talents of a student already in the library's employment to contribute to the instrument automation and design process. Never underestimate the skills and talents of those you work with on a daily basis.

TESTING BEFORE TESTING

A survey instrument must be thoroughly tested before it is deployed. Testing means checking not only that all the pages are displaying properly but that all of the potential responses are properly stored in the database. There are also compatibility issues with Internet browsers. Internet Explorer tolerates faulty HTML tags much better than Netscape does. Testing the instrument should also include determining how long it takes to complete the test.

DATA ANALYSIS

In order to tap the full potential of an automated survey instrument, an investigator should be able to ask complex questions such as: "How did female students, aged 18 to 20, born in the United States, with Spanish as a native language, respond to query #20?" A dynamic web-enabled tool should allow for precise results to any individual query, which could then be shared simultaneously with a wider audience. An added benefit of a web-enabled reporting tool is the ability to generate graphs. However, secure access to the results of any assessment might be needed in order to prevent unauthorized individuals from viewing data results.

Several commercial reporting tools are available, which allow the creation of customized reports with graphs from databases. However, a robust reporting tool can be developed with the web programming language used to automate the survey instrument and with freely available graphing software. The reporting tool for the *UMBC Survey* was built using PHP web programming language. This tool was connected to the database that stores the student responses. A free PHP software library called HTML Graphs was used to generate the graphs. Figure 10-1 is a screen shot of the user interface of the reporting tool developed for the *UMBC Survey*.

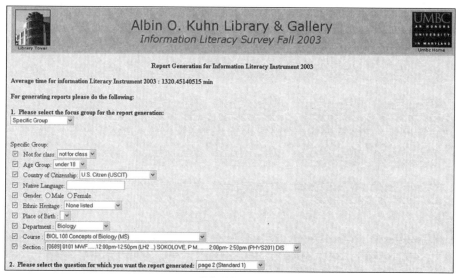

FIGURE 10-1
User (Researcher) Interface for Reporting Tool in the UMBC Survey

This reporting tool allowed the task force to identify a group within those surveyed and to correlate responses to queries for age, country of citizenship, native language, gender, ethnic heritage, and country of birth. Figure 10-2 shows the graphs generated in response to a query for a question in the *UMBC Survey*.

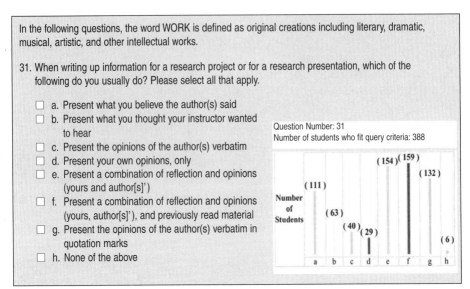

FIGURE 10-2
Graph Generated by Reporting Tool in the UMBC Survey

REPORTING TEXT FIELDS

Reporting the data from text fields creates a unique problem. With a text field, survey respondents can enter any text value in response to a particular query. This value may include spelling mistakes. The task force decided that all text fields in the *UMBC Survey* would be reported as they were submitted, with recurring identical text responses added to the list of responses for that item. For example, figure 10-3 shows responses to another query from the *UMBC Survey*: "Which Internet search engine do you use?"

Note the collapsing of the responses for Google (24) and the separate reporting of other "google" responses, although referring to the same search engine, as separate categories in the reporting tool. This method allows for all responses to be counted, regardless of spelling errors. Developing a reporting tool such as this significantly facilitates data analysis as well as graphical reports of that data—key concerns in assessment of any kind.

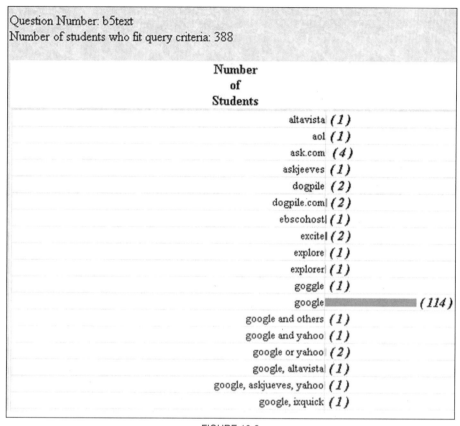

Question Number: b5text
Number of students who fit query criteria: 388

FIGURE 10-3
Text Response Generated by Reporting Tool in the UMBC Survey

REPORTING TO FACULTY

Figure 10-4 shows a reporting tool developed for the faculty that provides feedback regarding which students have taken the survey. This tool generates a list of the students that have taken the survey for a particular section. After selecting a department, class, and section, students are listed by their unique user name ID. This tool was particularly useful in that it allowed task force members to report to the faculty in a timely manner which students had participated in the *UMBC Survey*. Faculty members benefited from this tool since it enabled them to identify individual students to whom they could award extra credit for participating.

To generate a list of students that have taken the survey:

1. Select the department
2. Select the class
3. Select the section
4. Press the generate button
The list of the student's GL account usernames is generated.

Department: Psychology ▾

Course : PSYC 100 Introduction to Psychology (SS) ▾

Section and time : [4689] 0101 MWF.......9:00am-10:15am (LH1 ...) JORDAN, L ▾

GENERATE

LIST of GL Accounts of students for
Dept: Psychology
Course: PSYC 100 Introduction to Psychology (SS)
Section: [4689] 0101 MWF.......9:00am-10:15am (LH1 ...) JORDAN, L
who have taken the survey before: June 11, 2003

Student GL ID
major
sullivan
ahopki2

FIGURE 10-4
Reporting Tool Feedback for Faculty in the UMBC Survey

GLOSSARY

Active Server Pages (ASP). This technology can dynamically add, edit, or change the content of a web page and is similar to Java Server Pages but is Microsoft-based. ASP files usually run best on Microsoft's web server, Internet Information Service (IIS). An ASP file can contain text, HTML tags, and scripts.[4]

Apache Web server software. This software is a project aimed at developing and maintaining an open-source HTTP server for most operating systems, including UNIX and Windows NT. The goal of this project is to provide "a secure, efficient and extensible server that provides HTTP" web services in accordance with the current HTTP standards.[5] Another version of the Apache server called the Apache Tomcat web server can be used to implement Java Server Pages. For more information, see http://www.apache.org.

CGI/Perl. "CGI, or Common Gateway Interface, is the standard programming interface between Web servers and external programs" and a well-established technology for web interactivity. It is not a programming language itself but a standard method to allow external programs to run on a web server. "The CGI standard does not exist in isolation, it is dependent on the HTML and HTTP standards."[6] The external programs can be written in many languages, but the most common one is Perl. Perl is a high-level programming language with a great ability to process text. This functionality makes it an ideal web programming language. For more information, see http://www.perl.com.

DB2. This is a relational database developed by IBM that "provides a scalable, Web-ready database that delivers the performance, scalability, reliability, and availability needed for the most demanding eCommerce applications."[7] For more information, see http://www.ibm.com.

Microsoft Internet Information Service (IIS). This web server software is Microsoft-based and hence would not run on a Unix/Linux-based operating system. This software is included with all Windows NT, 2000, and XP operating systems. IIS supports dynamic (using ASP) as well as static web pages and provides full support to connect to external data sources such as Microsoft Access and Microsoft SQL Server.

MS SQL Server. Microsoft developed MS SQL Server as a high-performance database that can be used in place of Access databases for most applications. This server requires a Windows NT platform to run.

MySQL. This is the most popular open-source relational database management system. For more information, see http://www.mysql.com.

Oracle. When referring to an Oracle database, it is usually some version (8i or 9i) of Oracle's relational database system. "These databases are extremely robust, scalable and perform well with millions or billions of records."[8] For more information, see http://www.oracle.com

PHP. This is an open source web programming language that runs on most web servers. PHP is an acronym for "PHP: Hypertext Preprocessor." It is specifically designed for creating robust and reliable dynamic web pages for e-commerce and other web applications such as surveys.

Query. A query is a specific question submitted to the database requesting a particular response using data/values in a particular field or table.

NOTES

1. Polly Thistlethwaite et al., "The Data Game," http://manta.colostate.edu/datagame/. See also Polly J. Thistlethwaite, "The Data Game: Colorado State University's Animated Library Research Tool," *Colorado Libraries* 27, no. 3 (Fall 2001): 12–15.

2. Teresa Yvonne Neely, "Aspects of Information Literacy: A Sociological and Psychological Study (Ph.D. diss., University of Pittsburgh, 2000).

3. Chuck Newman, "Considering the Color-Blind," *New Architect Magazine*, no. 8, http://www.Webtechniques.com/archives/2000/08/newman/.

4. W3Schools, "ASP Tutorial: Introduction to ASP," http://www.w3schools.com/asp/asp_intro.asp.

5. Apache Software Foundation, "The Apache HTTP Server Project" (2003), http://httpd .apache.org/.

6. A. D. Marshall, "Practical Perl Programming," http://www.cs.cf.ac.uk/Dave/PERL/perl_caller.html.

7. IBM, "DB2 and Websphere MQ Integration (Part 1)," http://www7b.software.ibm .com/dmdd/library/tutorials/0210weinmeister/index.html.

8. SupportFreak.com, "Knowledge Base: What Is Oracle?" http://www.mysupportfreaks .com/cgi-bin/wsmkb.cgi?SHOW+22+Databases%7COracle#tops.

APPENDIX

Information Literacy Survey Instruments

Teresa Y. Neely

Auer, Nicole. *Research Skills Survey*. Virginia Polytechnic Institute and State University. See also Edward Lener, Susan Ariew, and Nancy Seamans, poster session at the Association of College and Research Libraries' 11th National Conference, "Learning to Make a Difference," Charlotte, NC, April 10–13, 2003.

Basic Skills Survey, Fall 2000. University of Charleston, WV.

Bay Area Community Colleges Assessment Project Team. *Bay Area Community Colleges Assessment Project: A Two-Part Information Competency Assessment Exam*. Bay Area Community Colleges Assessment Project, CA. http://www.topsy.org/ICAP/ICAProject.html. The Bay Area Community Colleges Assessment Project Team includes Bonnie Gratch-Lindauer, project leader, Pam Baker, Amelie Brown, Micca Gray, Andy Kivel, Brian Lym, and Topsy Smalley.

Berea College Evaluation. See under Henthorn, Susan, and Molly Royse.

Bissett, Susan, Genevieve Blake, Corinne Smith, E. K. Hawthorne, and J. Restrepo. *Union County College Library Pretest*. Union County College, NJ. http://faculty.ucc.edu/library/pretest.htm.

Black, Steve. *Assessment of Information Literacy Skills*. College of Saint Rose, NY. http://www.strose.edu/Library/bi/infolitres.htm.

Bobst Library's Information Literacy Quiz. New York University. Poster session at the Association of College and Research Libraries' 10th National Conference, "Crossing the Divide," Denver, March 15–18, 2001.

Bunz, Ulla K., and Howard E. Sypher. "The Computer-Email-Web (CEW) Fluency Scale—Development and Validation." Presentation at the National Communications Association Conference, Atlanta, November 1–4, 2001. ERIC ED 458 657. See also Ulla Bunz, "The Computer-Email-Web (CEW) Fluency Scale—Development and Validation," *International Journal of Human-Computer Interaction* 17, no. 4 (2004): 479–506.

Cal Poly–Pomona Information Competency Assessment. See under Dunn, Kathleen.

Campbell-Meier, Jennifer, and Lea Simon. *LIBM 155 Pre-Test.* Northern State University, SD. Poster session at the Association of College and Research Libraries' 11th National Conference, "Learning to Make a Difference," Charlotte, NC, April 10–13, 2003.

Caravello, Patti S., Eloisa Gomez Borah, Judith Herschman, and Eleanor Mitchell. University of California, Los Angeles. *UCLA Library Instructional Services Advisory Committee Questionnaire.* In "Information Competence at UCLA: Report of a Survey Project," April 1, 2001. http://repositories.cdlib.org/uclalib/il/01/.

CGA Skills Assessment. See under Daragan, Patricia, and Gwendolyn Stevens.

Clarke, Tobin. *Information Competency Assessment Instrument.* California State University, Dominguez Hills. http://library.csudh.edu/infocomp/quiz.html.

Computer and Information Literacy Self-Assessment Survey. Old Dominion University, VA. http://www.odu.edu/webroot/orgs/AO/CLT/FAssess.nsf/Computer_Information_Literacy_Survey?OpenForm.

Congrove, Angela. "Survey of College Students regarding Copyright Law Information." Otterbein College, OH. http://www.otterbein.edu/surveys/copyright/.

Cornell Computer Skills Survey. See under Ochs, Mary, Bill Coons, Darla Van Ostrand, and Susan Barnes.

Costantino, Connie Ellen. *Student Survey/Faculty and Administrator Survey and Student Interview/Faculty and Administrator Interview.* In Connie E. Costantino, "Stakeholders' Perceptions of the Importance of Information Literacy Competencies within Undergraduate Education" (Ed.D. diss., Alliant International University, CA, 2003).

Cox, Suellen, and Patricia Szeszulski. *Assessing Information Competence across Disciplines.* California State University, Fullerton. http://guides.library.fullerton.edu/infocomp/index.htm; http://faculty.fullerton.edu/ scox/.

CSU Minimum Competency Survey. See under Mach, Michelle, Jennifer Kutzik, Teresa Neely, Kevin Cullen, and Lindsey Wess.

Daniels, Kathleen, Thomas Eland, Virginia Heinrich, Jane Jurgens, Anne Ryan, and Julie Setnosky. *INFS 1000, Information Literacy Mid-Term Exam with ACRL Objectives for Information Literacy Instruction; INFS 1000 Information Literacy Competency Exam with ACRL Objectives for Information Literacy Instruction; Pre-Test.* Minneapolis Community and Technical College. http://db.mctc.mnscu.edu/library/courses/infs1000/assessment/MidTermExam.pdf.

Daragan, Patricia, and Gwendolyn Stevens. *Coast Guard Academy Library Research Skills Assessment, 1995, 1996.* See also Patricia Daragan and Gwendolyn Stevens, "Developing Lifelong Learners: An Integrative and Developmental Approach to Information Literacy." *Research Strategies* 14, no. 2 (1996): 68–81.

Davis, Hazel. *Information Literacy Quiz.* Rio Salado College, AZ. http://www.rio.maricopa.edu/services/student/support/library/test_yourself_quiz.shtml.

De Jong, Mark. *Information Literacy Survey.* Frostburg State University, MD.

DeArmond, Celita. *Questions from Your Friendly Reference Librarian.* University of Texas, San Antonio. 1998.

Drew, Christine. *Information Literacy Assessment Form.* George C. Gordon Library, Worcester Polytechnic Institute, MA.

Dunn, Kathleen. *Information Competency Assessment.* California Polytechnic State University, Pomona. http://www.csupomona.edu/~library/InfoComp/instrument.htm.

East Carolina University, Joyner Library Reference Department. *Background Information Quiz.* http://www.lib.ecu.edu/Reference/workshop/back.htm.

———. *Can't Think of a Topic Quiz.* http://www.lib.ecu.edu/Reference/workshop/canatthink.htm.

———. *Choose Your Topic Quiz.* http://www.lib.ecu.edu/Reference/workshop/topic.htm.

———. *Find Books on Your Topic Quiz.* http://www.lib.ecu.edu/Reference/workshop/catalogc.htm.

———. *Finding Articles Quiz.* http://www.lib.ecu.edu/Reference/workshop/articles.htm.

———. *Library Instruction Quiz.* http://lib.edu.edu/Reference/Instruction/quizc.htm.

Eckman, Catherine. *Pretest/Post Test.* Midlands Technical College, SC. Poster session at the Association of College and Research Libraries' 11th

National Conference, "Learning to Make a Difference," Charlotte, NC, April 10–13, 2003.

Elteto, Sharon. *Information Literacy Inventory.* Portland State University, OR. http://www.lib.pdx.edu/instruction/infoliteracy.html.

FGC Skunk Ape Tutorial. See under Florida Gulf Coast University Library.

Florida Gulf Coast University Library, Research Services Department. *Search for the Skunk Ape (Information Literacy Tutorial).* http://ruby.fgcu.edu/courses/cslater/skunkape/instructions.htm.

Geffert, Bryn, and Robert Bruce. *Library Bibliographic Instruction Survey.* St. Olaf College, MN. In Bryn Geffert and Robert Bruce, "Whither BI? Assessing Perceptions of Research Skills over an Undergraduate Career," *RQ* 36, no. 3 (Spring 1997): 409–17.

Geffert, Bryn, and Beth Christensen. *Week One Library Survey.* St. Olaf College, MN. In Bryn Geffert and Beth Christensen, "Things They Carry: Attitudes toward, Opinions about, and Knowledge of Libraries and Research among Incoming College Students," *Reference and User Services Quarterly* 37, no. 3 (Spring 1998): 279–89.

Georgetown College Task-Based Technology Assessment Test. See under Rafaill, William S., and Andrea C. Peach.

Gratch-Lindauer, Bonnie, et al. See under Bay Area Community Colleges Assessment Project Team.

Henthorn, Susan, and Molly Royse. *Bibliographic Instruction Program Evaluation, Hutchins Library Inventory.* Berea College, KY. http://faculty.berea.edu/henthorns/bieval/.

Hime, Laurie H. *Library Research Assignment.* Miami-Dade College, Kendall. http://www.mdcc.edu/kendall/library/ht_2004.htm.

Information Competency Assessment Instrument. See under Clarke, Tobin.

Information Literacy Assessment (Cabrillo College). See under Smalley, Topsy.

Information Literacy Assessment. Rappahannock Community College, VA. http://www.rccl.cc.va.us/public/library/assessment.html.

Information Literacy Evaluation. Harford Community College, MD. http://www.harford.edu/faculty/lheil/information_literacy_assessment.asp.

Information Literacy Pre-Test for ISO 201. See under Schroeder, Randall, Jill Gremmels, and Karen Lehmann.

Information Literacy Survey. (Franklin and Marshall College, PA.) Samford University, AL. http://library.samford.edu/about/li/infolit/example1.htm.

Information Literacy Test, Spring 2005. Thomas Tredway Library, Augustana College, IL.

Jackman, Lana Webb. *Information Resources Survey*. In Lana Webb Jackman, "Information Literacy: An Issue of Equity for the New Majority Student" (Ph.D. diss., Lesley College, MA, 1999).

Kirby, R. Kenneth, and Don Wilson. *Samford University Arts and Sciences Critical Competencies Project*. Samford University, AL. http://library.samford.edu/about/li/infolit/example10.htm.

Libutti, Patricia. *Education Information Literacy Self Report*. Fordham University, NY. In Patricia Libutti, "Library Support for Graduate Education Research and Teaching" (April 1991), ERIC ED 349 007.

Linhart, Rod. *Information Literacy Skills—Assess*. University of Southern Queensland, Australia.

———. *Information Literacy Skills—Defining Skills*. University of Southern Queensland, Australia.

———. *Information Literacy Skills—Locating Skills*. University of Southern Queensland, Australia.

———. *Information Literacy Skills—Organise and Present*. University of Southern Queensland, Australia.

———. *Information Literacy Skills—Selection*. University of Southern Queensland, Australia.

List-Handley, Carla. *LIB Proficiency Exam*. State University of New York, Plattsburgh.

Lowell, N., G. Bunker, J. McKinstry, and D. E. McGhee. *Information Literacy (General Studies 391)*. Winter and Spring, 1998. University of Washington. OEA Report 98-10. http://www.washington.edu/oea/9810.htm.

Luévano, S., T. Travis, and E. Wakiji. *Information Competence Tutorial Pre-Test*. Black Studies, California State University, Long Beach. http://www.csulb.edu/~ttravis/IC/CSULB/pretest.htm. See also Information Competence for Chicano and Latino Studies. http://www.csulb.edu/~sluevano/chls/.

Mach, Michelle, Jennifer Kutzik, Teresa Neely, Kevin Cullen, and Lindsey Wess. *CSU Libraries Minimum Competency Survey*. Colorado State University. Working paper. 2003.

Maryville Inventory. See under Nugent, Christine.

Maughan, Patricia Davitt. *Teaching Library History 7B Pre- and Post-Test. Information Literacy Survey, Spring 1994/History 7B Pre-Test*. Spring 1996, Spring 1997, and Fall 1999. Teaching Library, University of California, Berkeley. http://www.lib.berkeley.edu/AboutLibrary/Staff/CUNews/cu_071599.html#tlib; http://www.lib.berkeley.edu/Teaching

Lib/Survey.html. See also Patricia Davitt Maughan, "Assessing Information Literacy among Undergraduates: A Discussion of the Literature and the University of California–Berkeley Assessment Experience," *College and Research Libraries* 62, no. 1 (January 2001): 71–85

Moore, Anne Cooper. *New Mexico State University Information Literacy Instrument.* In Anne Cooper Moore, "The Impact of Hands-on Information Literacy Instruction on Learning/Knowledge of Information Literacy Concepts and Mastery of the Research Process in College Courses: A Quasi-Experimental Study" (Ph.D. diss., New Mexico State University, 2002). Dissertation Abstracts International, 62/11, 3610.

Morner, Claudia J. *Morner Test of Library Research Skills.* In Claudia J. Morner, "A Test of Library Research Skills for Education Doctoral Students" (Ph.D. diss., Boston College, 1993).

Mulherrin, Elizabeth. *COMM 393 Library Instruction Pre-Test/Post Test.* Information and Library Services, University of Maryland University College. October 2003.

Neely, Teresa Yvonne. *Neely Test of Relevance, Evaluation, and Information Literacy Attitudes.* In Teresa Yvonne Neely, "Aspects of Information Literacy: A Sociological and Psychological Study" (Ph.D. diss., University of Pittsburgh, 2000).

Nero, Lut Rahim. *Information Literacy Assessment.* Milliken University. In Lut Rahim Nero, "An Assessment of Information Literacy among Graduating Teacher Education Majors of Four Pennsylvania State System of Higher Education (SSHE) Universities" (Ph.D. diss., University of Pittsburgh, 1999).

New Mexico State University Information Literacy Instrument. See under Moore, Anne Cooper.

Nugent, Christine. *Information Literacy Competency Inventory (Pretest)— 2001/2002.* Maryville College, TN. Poster session at the Association of College and Research Libraries' 11th National Conference, "Learning to Make a Difference," Charlotte, NC, April 10–13, 2003. http://www.warren-wilson.edu/~library/acrl.htm. This survey instrument was produced by Roger Myers, Maryville College.

Ochs, Mary, Bill Coons, Darla Van Ostrand, and Susan Barnes. *Computer Skills for Information Retrieval and Management: A Survey of the Skills of Selected Cornell University Business and Finance Graduates.* In Mary Ochs, Bill Coons, Darla Van Ostrand, and Susan Barnes, "Assessing the

Value of an Information Literacy Program" (October 1991), ERIC ED 340 385.

Palmer, Olia, and Sarah Naper. *Principles of Sociology—Information Retrieval and Evaluation Quiz*. Fall 2001. University of Northern Colorado. Research conducted at North Harris College, TX. Poster session at the Association of College and Research Libraries' 11th National Conference, "Learning to Make a Difference," Charlotte, NC, April 10–13, 2003.

Payton, Annie Malessia Nash. *Faculty Perception Survey of Information Literacy Skills*. In Annie Malessia Nash Payton, "Self-Reported Perceptions of Literacy Skills in Nursing Programs at Selected Southern Institutions" (Ph.D. diss., University of Southern Mississippi, 2003).

Pierce, Susan Tatum. *Ranking Instrument*. In Susan Tatum Pierce, "Readiness for Evidence-Based Practice: Information Literacy Needs of Nursing Faculty and Students in a Southern United States State" (Ed.D. diss., Northwestern State University of Louisiana, 2000). See also A. B. Tanner, "Readiness for Evidence-Based Practice: Information Literacy Needs of Nursing Faculty and Students in a Southern United States State" (Ed.D. diss., Northwestern State University of Louisiana, 2000); and D. S. Pravikoff, S. Pierce, and A. B. Tanner, "Are Nurses Ready for Evidence-Based Practice?: A Study Suggests That Greater Support Is Needed," *AJN: American Journal of Nursing* 103, no. 5 (May 2003): 95–96.

Powell, Carol A., and Jane Case-Smith. *Occupational Therapy Graduates Survey*. Ohio State University. In Carol A. Powell and Jane Case-Smith, "Information Literacy Skills of Occupational Therapy Graduates: A Survey of Learning Outcomes," *Journal of the Medical Library Association* 91, no. 4 (October 2003): 468–77.

Rafaill, William S., and Andrea C. Peach. *Georgetown College Task-Based Technology Assessment Test*. Georgetown College, KY. In William S. Rafaill and Andrea C. Peach, "Are Your Students Ready for College? Technology Literacy at Georgetown College" (2001), ERIC ED 463 728.

Ranadive, Mary, Regina Rose, Sara Crest, and Mary Volland. *Whaddyaknow*. Towson University, MD. http://pages.towson.edu/ranadive/pre_spring _assessment_2004.htm.

Readel, Karin. *UMBC Information Technology Awareness Questionnaire/ SCI 100 Spring 2003*. © 1999–2005 Karin E. Readel. All rights reserved. University of Maryland, Baltimore County. UMBC Office of Information Technology, Brown Bag Series. http:/www.umbc.edu/oit/training/itaq/ itaq.html.

Saint Rose Assessment. See under Black, Steve.

Schroeder, Randall, Jill Gremmels, and Karen Lehmann. *Information Literacy Pre-Test for IS 201.* Fall 2004. Wartburg College, IA. http://public .wartburg.edu/library/infolit/assessment.html.

Seamans, Nancy H. *Questions Distributed to Student Participants via Email/ Questions That Were Included on the Annual Freshman Survey, Summer 2000.* In Nancy H. Seamans, "Information Literacy: A Study of Freshman Students' Perceptions, with Recommendations" (Ph.D. diss., Virginia Polytechnic Institute and State University, 2001).

Shane, Jordana M. Y. *Information Literacy Assessment for First-Year Students.* Fall 2000. Philadelphia University, PA. http://www.philau.edu/ library/infolit/.

Silver, Susan, and Lisa Nickel. *Library Instruction Pre- and Post-Test.* University of South Florida. Poster session at the American Library Association's Annual Conference, Atlanta, June 13–19, 2002. http://www .lib.usf.edu/~nickel/handout.htm.

Smalley, Topsy. *Information Literacy Assessment.* Cabrillo College, CA. http: //topsy.org/ICAP/ICAProject.html.

South Seattle Community College Instructional Resources Library User Survey. In South Seattle Community College, "South Seattle Community College Instructional Resources Library User Study" (March 1993), ERIC ED 381 217.

Stern, Caroline Marie. *Ferris State University, 2001 Orientation Survey.* In Caroline Marie Stern, "Assessing Entry-Level Digital Information Literacy of In-Coming College Freshmen" (Ph.D. diss., Capella University, MN, 2002).

Stoner, Connie Salyers, Mary Cummings, and Ann Marie Short. *Assessment of Information Literacy.* Shawnee State University, OH. http://www .shawnee.edu/off/cml/litsurv111.html.

Student Information Literacy Survey. Mount St. Mary's College, CA. http: //www.msmc.la.edu/library/infolilt/stulit.htm.

Survey of College Students regarding Copyright Law Information. See under Congrove, Angela.

Swart, William J., and Lisa M. Brunick. *SOCI 300: Social Psychology, Student Evaluation B Pre-Test, Student Evaluation Post-Test.* Augustana College, IL. http://www.mnprivatecolleges.com/binaries/flip_augustana2.pdf.

UC Berkeley Pretest. See under Maughan, Patricia Davitt.

UCLA Library Instructional Services Advisory Committee Questionnaire. See under Caravello, Patti S., Eloisa Gomez Borah, Judith Herschman, and Eleanor Mitchell.

UMBC Information Literacy Task Force. *Albin O. Kuhn Library & Gallery Information Literacy Survey, 2003.* University of Maryland, Baltimore County. http://aok.lib.umbc.edu/reference/InformationLiteracy/umbc survey.pdf.

UMBC Survey. See under UMBC Information Literacy Task Force.

UNM Education Information Literacy Pre-Test, 2006. University Libraries and the College of Education, University of New Mexico. Developed by Teresa Y. Neely, Mark Emmons, Elizabeth Keefe, Kate Luger, and Michele Mals.

UW Information Literacy questionnaire. See under Lowell, N., G. Bunker, J. McKinstry, and D. E. McGhee.

Van Scoyoc, Anna M. *Test Instrument.* University of Georgia. In Anna M. Van Scoyoc, "Reducing Library Anxiety in First-Year Students: The Impact of Computer-Assisted Instruction and Bibliographic Instruction," *Reference and User Services Quarterly* 42, no. 4 (Summer 2003): 329–41. Derived from Sharon L. Bostick, "The Development and Validation of the Library Anxiety Scale" (Ph.D. diss., Wayne State University, MI, 1992).

Vickery, Susan, and Heather Cooper. *Information Literacy and Information Technology Skills Audit.* Macquarie University, Australia. In Susan Vickery and Heather Cooper, "Confidence or Competence? Auditing Information Literacy Skills of Biology Undergraduate Students." http:// www.lib.mq.edu.au/conference/educause/competence.pdf.

BIBLIOGRAPHY
Katy Sullivan

ACRL Task Force on Information Literacy Competency Standards. "Information Literacy Competency Standards for Higher Education: The Final Version, Approved January 2000." *College and Research Libraries News* 61, no. 3 (March 2000): 207–15.

Apache Software Foundation. "The Apache HTTP Server Project." 2003. http://httpd.apache.org/.

Association of College and Research Libraries. "Characteristics of Programs of Information Literacy That Illustrate Best Practice." *College and Research Libraries News* 64, no. 1 (January 2003): 32–35.

———. "Information Literacy: The Standards Step-by-Step: Standard Five." http://www.ala.org/ala/acrl/acrlissues/acrlinfolit/infolitstandards/stepbystep1/stepby step.htm#standard5.

———. "Objectives for Information Literacy Instruction: A Model Statement for Academic Librarians." http://www.ala.org/ala/acrl/acrlstandards/objectivesinfor mation.htm.

———. "Standards and Guidelines." http://www.ala.org/ala/acrl/acrlstandards/standards guidelines.htm.

Atkinson, Joseph, and Miguel Figueroa. "Information Seeking Behavior of Business Students: A Research Study." *Reference Librarian* 58 (1997): 59–73.

Bales, Jack. "History 299 Materials: The Library and the Research Log." University of Mary Washington, VA. http://www.mwc.edu/hisa/resources/writing/299/research log_299.htm.

Bay Area Community Colleges Assessment Project Team. *Bay Area Community Colleges Assessment Project: A Two-Part Information Competency Assessment Exam.* Bay Area Community Colleges Assessment Project, CA. http://www.topsy.org/ICAP/ICAProject.html. The Bay Area Community Colleges Assessment Project Team includes Bonnie Gratch-Lindauer, project leader, Pam Baker, Amelie Brown, Micca Gray, Andy Kivel, Brian Lym, and Topsy Smalley.

Beck, Susan E. "LSC 311 Information Literacy, Hands-on #5: Finding Periodicals and Using Print Periodical Indexes. Subject Headings Change Over Time." New Mexico State University. http://lib.nmsu.edu/intruction/lsc311/beck/assign05.html.

Beno, Barbara A. "The Role of Student Learning Outcomes in Accreditation Quality Review." *New Directions for Community Colleges*, no. 126 (Summer 2004): 65.

Berman, Sanford. *Prejudices and Antipathies: A Tract on the LC Subject Heads concerning People.* Metuchen, NJ: Scarecrow, 1971.

Betz, A. L., John J. Skowronski, and Thomas M. Ostrom. "Shared Realities: Social Influence and Stimulus Memory." *Social Cognition* 14, no. 2 (1996): 113–14.

Blakeslee, Sarah. "UNIV001C: Introduction to University Life Information Competency Assignment: Choosing the Right Database." California State University, Chico. http://www.csuchico.edu/lins/IC_grant/sample_assignments/Choosing_Right_Database.doc.

Boston, Carol. "The Concept of Formative Assessment." *Practical Assessment, Research and Evaluation* 8, no. 9 (2002). http://pareonline.net/getvn.asp?v=8&n=9/.

Brainard, Sue Ann. "Search Scenario." State University of New York, Geneseo. http://library.geneseo.edu/~brainard/chapters.htm.

Brainard, Sue Ann, Trudi Jacobson, and Timothy Gatti, eds. *Teaching Information Literacy Concepts: Activities and Frameworks from the Field.* Pittsburgh: Library Instruction, 2001.

Buchanan, Lori, Ted Jones, and DeAnne Luck. "Collaborating Online to Teach Information and Multimedia Literacy." Austin Peay State University, TN. Paper presented at the Seventh Annual Mid-South Instructional Technology Conference, "Teaching, Learning, and Technology: The Connected Classroom," Murfreesboro, TN, April 7–9, 2002. http://www.mtsu.edu/~itconf/proceed02/50.html.

Bunz, Ulla "The Computer-Email-Web (CEW) Fluency Scale—Development and Validation." *International Journal of Human-Computer Interaction* 17, no. 4 (2004): 479–506.

Bunz, Ulla K., and Howard E. Sypher. "The Computer-Email-Web (CEW) Fluency Scale—Development and Validation." Presentation at the National Communications Association Conference, Atlanta, November 1–4, 2001, ERIC ED 458 657.

Central Queensland University Library, Australia. "Assessment Ideas." http://www
.library.cqu.edu.au/informationliteracy/teachresources/assess_list.htm.
———. "Information Literacy at CQU." http://www.library.cqu.edu.au/information
literacy/teachresources/resources4standards.html.
———. "Search Strategy Paraphrase." http://www.library.cqu.edu.au/information
literacy/teachresources/assess_ideas.htm.
———. "What to Do When the Book You Want Isn't Available." http://www.library
.cqu.edu.au/compass/find/book_not_available.htm.
Colorado State University, Office of Admissions. "Black Issues Forum." http://lib
.colostate.edu/research/divandarea/bif/.
Conderman, Greg, and Carol Koroghlanian. "Writing Test Questions like a Pro."
Intervention in School and Clinic 38, no. 2 (November 2002): 83–87.
Congrove, Angela. "Survey of College Students regarding Copyright Law Information."
Otterbein College, OH. 2004. http://www.otterbein.edu/surveys/copyright/.
Constantino, Connie E. "Stakeholders' Perceptions of the Importance of Informa-
tion Literacy Competencies within Undergraduate Education." Ed.D. diss.,
Alliant International University, CA, 2003.
Cothey, Vivian. "A Longitudinal Study of World Wide Web Users' Information-
Searching Behavior." *Journal of American Society for Information Science and
Technology* 53, no. 2 (1992): 67–78.
Crown, Deborah F., and M. Shane Spiller. "Learning from the Literature on Colle-
giate Cheating: A Review of Empirical Research." *Journal of Business Ethics* 17
(1998): 383–90.
Daragan, Patricia, and Gwendolyn Stevens. "Developing Lifelong Learners: An Inte-
grative and Developmental Approach to Information Literacy." *Research Strate-
gies* 14, no. 2 (1996): 68–81.
Davis, Philip M. "Effect of the Web on Undergraduate Citation Behavior: Guiding
Student Scholarship in a Networked Age." *Portal: Libraries and the Academy* 3,
no. 1 (2003): 41–51.
Doyle, Christina S. "Development of a Model of Information Literacy Outcome
Measures within the National Education Goals of 1990." Ph.D. diss., Northern
Arizona University, 1992.
Dunn, Kathleen. "Information Competency Assessment: Web-Based Assessment of
University Entry-Level Information Competency." June 1999. http://www
.csupomona.edu/~library/InfoComp/.
Eberhardt, Thomas. *E-literate?* Videocassette. Los Angeles: Pacific Bell/University
of California, Los Angeles, Graduate School of Education and Information
Studies, 2000.
Educational Multimedia Fair Use Guidelines Development Committee. "Fair Use
Guidelines for Educational Multimedia." 1996. http://www.oit.cmich.edu/it/
policies_multi_fairuse.asp.

Educational Testing Service. "ETS ICT Literacy Assessment Premieres at Portland State University: New Test Measures Students' Ability to Process and Communicate Information in a Technological Environment." March 3, 2005. http://www.ets.org/ictliteacy/05030901.html.

———. "ETS Launches ICT Literacy Assessment, an Online Measure of Student Information and Communication Technology Proficiency." November 8, 2004. http://www.ets.org/ictliteracy/educator.html.

———. *ICT Literacy Assessment: Do Your Students Have the ICT Skills They Need to Succeed?* Brochure, 2005.

Feinberg, Richard. "Citation Analysis." http://library.morrisville.edu/sunyla/lic/SCLD.html.

Flaspohler, Molly R. "Information Literacy Program Assessment: One Small College Takes the Big Plunge." *Reference Services Review* 31, no. 2 (2003): 129–40.

Foster, Andrea L. "Lawmakers Demand That Colleges Crack Down on Illegal File Sharing." *Chronicle of Higher Education*, Information Technology, February 27, 2003. http://chronicle.com/free/2003/02/2003022701t.htm.

Franklyn-Stokes, Arlene, and Stephen E. Newstead. "Undergraduate Cheating: Who Does What and Why." *Studies in Higher Education* 20, no. 2 (June 1995): 159–72.

Gaddis, Susanne E. "How to Design Online Surveys." *Training and Development* 15, no. 6 (June 1998): 67–71.

Geffert, Bryn, and Beth Christensen. "Things They Carry: Attitudes toward, Opinions about, and Knowledge of Libraries and Research among Incoming College Students." *Reference and User Services Quarterly* 37, no. 3 (1998): 279–89.

Geoghegan, Andy. "Critical Thinking across the Curriculum Project: Critical Thinking Psychology Exercises, Jumping to Conclusions." Longview Community College, MO. http://www.kcmetro.cc.mo.us/longview/ctac/psychexer1.htm.

Greer, Arlene, Lee Weston, and Mary Alm. "Assessment of Learning Outcomes: A Measure of Progress in Library Literacy." *College and Research Libraries* 52, no. 6 (1991): 549–57.

Hinman, Sheryl. "Analyzing Copyright in the Technology World." *Update on Law-Related Education* 22, no. 2 (1998): 46–50.

Howard, Rebecca Moore. "Plagiarisms, Authorships, and the Academic Death Penalty." *College English* 57, no. 7 (1995): 788–806.

———. *Standing in the Shadow of Giants: Plagiarists, Authors, Collaborators.* Stamford, CT: Ablex, 1999.

Humboldt State University Library. "Journals—Scholarly or Popular?" http://library.humboldt.edu/infoservices/scholorpop.htm.

Hurlbert, Janet McNeil, Cathleen R. Savidge, and Georgia R. Laudenslager. "Process-Based Assignments: How Promoting Information Literacy Prevents Plagiarism." *College and Undergraduate Libraries* 10, no. 1 (2003): 39–51.

IBM. "DB2 and Websphere MQ Integration (Part 1)." http://www7b.software.ibm .com/dmdd/library/tutorials/0210weinmeister/index.html.

Illing, Patty, and Michael Connelly. "Critical Thinking across the Curriculum Project: Facts, Opinions, and Reasoned Judgments." Longview Community College, MO. http://www.kcmetro.cc.mo.us/longview/ctac/opinion.htm.

Indiana University Bloomington Libraries, Assessment Planning Committee. "An Assessment Plan for Information Literacy (Final)." 1996. http://www.indiana .edu/~libinstr/Information_Literacy/assessment.html.

Johnson, Kristin. "UNIV001C: Introduction to University Life Information Competency Assignment, Using the Library of Congress Subject Headings (LCSH)." Meriam Library, California State University, Chico. http://www .csuchico.edu/lins/IC_grant/sample_assignments/LC_Subject_Headings.doc.

Johnson, M. K., S. Hastroudi, and D. S. Lindsay. "Source Monitoring." *Psychological Bulletin* 114, no. 3 (1993): 3–28.

Joseph, Miriam E. "Term Paper Alternative or . . . So You'd Like Your Students to Use the Library but Don't Want to Assign a Research Paper?" Pius XII Memorial Library, Saint Louis University, MO. 1992. http://www.lib.berkeley.edu/ TeachingLib/PaperAlternatives.html.

Kapitzke, Cushla. "Information Literacy: A Positivist Epistemology and a Politics of *Out*formation." *Educational Theory* 53, no. 1 (Winter 2003): 37–53.

Kelley, Kimberly E. "Information Literacy and Writing Assessment Project: Tutorial for Developing and Evaluating Assignments." Information and Library Services, University of Maryland University College. http://www.umuc.edu/library/ tutorials/information_literacy/sect4.html#sample.

Kivel, Andy. "Designing and Field Testing an Information Competency Proficiency Exam for California Community Colleges." Poster session at the Association of College and Research Libraries' 11th National Conference, "Learning to Make a Difference," Charlotte, NC, April 10–13, 2003.

Kuhlthau, Carol C. "Developing a Model of the Library Search Process: Cognitive and Affective Aspects." *Reference Quarterly* 28 (1988): 232–42.

———. "Information Search Process: A Summary of Research and Implications for School Library Media Programs." *School Library Media Quarterly* 18 (1989): 19–25.

———. "Inside the Search Process: Information Seeking from the User's Perspective." *Journal of the American Society for Information Science* 42 (1991): 361–71.

Labelle, Patrick R. "Designing Meaningful Library Assignments—Writing a Family History." Concordia University Libraries, Quebec. http://library.concordia.ca/ services/users/faculty/assignment.html.

Macrae, C. Neil, Galen V. Bodenhausen, and Guglielmo Calvini. "Contexts of Cryptomnesia: May the Source Be with You." *Social Cognition* 17 (1999): 273–97.

Manning, Melissa Ann. "Cheating, Anomie and Academic Ethics." Ph.D. diss., University of Kansas, 1994.

Mark, Beth L. "Creating Newsletters." Messiah College Library, PA. http://library
.morrisville.edu/sunyla/lic/SCLD.html.

Marshall, A. D. "Practical Perl Programming." http://www.cs.cf.ac.uk/Dave/PERL/
perl_caller.html.

Maughan, Patricia Davitt. "Assessing Information Literacy among Undergraduates:
A Discussion of the Literature and the University of California–Berkeley Assessment Experience." *College and Research Libraries* 62, no. 1 (January 2001):
71–85.

McCabe, Donald L. "Faculty Responses to Academic Dishonesty: The Influence of
Student Honor Codes." *Research in Higher Education* 34, no. 5 (1993): 647–59.

McCabe, Donald, and Patrick Drinan. "Toward a Culture of Academic Integrity."
Chronicle of Higher Education 46, no. 8 (1999): B7.

McCabe, Donald, and Linda Klebe Trevino. "Individual and Contextual Influences
on Academic Dishonesty: A Multicampus Investigation." *Research in Higher
Education* 38, no. 3 (1997): 379–97.

McCabe, Donald, Linda Klebe Trevino, and Kenneth D. Butterfield. "Academic
Integrity in Honor Code and Non-Honor Code Environments." *Journal of
Higher Education* 70, no. 2 (1999): 211–35.

———. "Cheating in Academic Institutions: A Decade of Research." *Ethics and Behavior* 11, no. 3 (2001): 219–33.

———. "Dishonesty in Academic Environments: The Influence of Peer Reporting
Requirements." *Journal of Higher Education* 72, no. 1 (2001): 29–45.

McCollum, Kelley, and Peter Schmidt. "How Forcefully Should Universities Enforce Copyright Law on Audio Files?" *Chronicle of Higher Education* 46, no. 13
(1999): A59–60.

Memorial University of Newfoundland, Memorial University Libraries. "Ideas for
Library/Information Assignments." http://www.library.mun.ca/qeii/instruction/
assignment_ideas.php.

Middle States Commission on Higher Education. *Characteristics of Excellence in
Higher Education*. Philadelphia: Middle States Commission on Higher Education, 2002. http://www.msache.org.

———. *Developing Research and Communication Skills: Guidelines for Information
Literacy in the Curriculum*. Philadelphia: Middle States Commission on Higher
Education, 2003.

Minneapolis Community and Technical College. "Information Literacy and Research Skills—INFS 1000." http://db.mctc.mnscu.edu/library/courses/infs
1000/infs1000.htm.

Morner, Claudia J. "A Test of Library Research Skills for Education Doctoral
Students." Ph.D. diss., Boston College, 1993.

Morrison, Heather. "Information Literacy Skills: An Exploratory Focus Group Study
of Student Perceptions." *Research Strategies* 15, no. 1 (1997): 4–17.

Neely, Teresa Yvonne. "Aspects of Information Literacy: A Sociological and Psychological Study." Ph.D. diss., University of Pittsburgh, 2000.

———. *Sociological and Psychological Aspects of Information Literacy in Higher Education.* Lanham, MD: Scarecrow, 2002.

———. "Using Subject Terminology and Classification to Provide Effective Service to Diverse Populations." *Colorado Libraries* 21, no. 2 (Summer 1995): 22–26.

Nelson, William N., and Robert W. Fernekes. "Who Uses ACRL Standards?" *College and Research Libraries News* 66, no. 5 (May 2005): 359–64.

Nero, Lut Rahim. "An Assessment of Information Literacy among Graduating Teacher Education Majors of Four Pennsylvania State System of Higher Education (SSHE) Universities." Ph.D. diss., University of Pittsburgh, 1999.

Newman, Chuck. "Considering the Color-Blind." *New Architect Magazine*, no. 8. http://www.Webtechniques.com/archives/2000/08/newman/.

O'Connor, Lisa G., Carolyn J. Radcliff, and Julie A. Gedeon. "Applying Systems Design and Item Response Theory to the Problem of Measuring Information Literacy Skills." *College and Research Libraries* 63, no. 6 (November 2002): 528–43. See also http://www.projectsails.org.

Old Dominion University. "Computer and Information Literacy Self-Assessment Survey." http://www.odu.edu/webroot/orgs/AO/CLT/FAssess.nsf/Computer_Information_Literacy_Survey?OpenForm.

Park, Chris. "In Other (People's) Words: Plagiarism by University Students—Literature and Lessons." *Assessment and Evaluation in Higher Education* 28, no. 5 (2003): 471–88.

Parker-Gibson, Necia. "Library Assignments: Challenges That Students Face and How to Help." *College Teaching* 49, no. 2 (2001): 65.

Payne, Kathy. "Using *InfoTrac SearchBank* and Using Yahoo." Stewart Library Information Literacy Team, Weber State University, UT. http://myhome.sunyocc.edu/~weilera/lic/SCLD.html.

Pennycook, Alastair. "Borrowing Others' Words: Text, Ownership, Memory, and Plagiarism." *TESOL Quarterly* 30, no. 2 (1996): 201–30.

Pimple, Kenneth D. "Using Case Studies in Teaching Research Ethics." 2003. http://poynter.indiana.edu/tre/kdp-cases.pdf.

Powell, Carol A., and Jane Case-Smith. "Information Literacy Skills of Occupational Therapy Graduates: A Survey of Learning Outcomes." *Journal of the Medical Library Association* 91, no. 4 (October 2003): 468–78.

Rafaill, William S., and Andrea C. Peach. "Are Your Students Ready for College? Technology Literacy at Georgetown College." In Proceedings of the Annual Mid-South Instructional Technology Conference, Murfreesboro, TN, April 8–10, 2001, ERIC ED 463 728.

Reed, Jeffrey G. "Information-Seeking Behavior of College Students Using a Library to Do Research: A Pilot Study." 1974. ERIC ED 100 306.

Register.com. "Domain Name Rules." http://www.register.com.

Reitz, Joan. "LC Call Number Quiz." Western Connecticut State University Library. http://www.wcsu.edu/library/lc_quiz.html.

Repman, Judi, and Elizabeth Downs. "Policy Issues for the 21st Century Library Media Center." *Book Report* 17, no. 5 (March/April 1999): 8–11.

Ricigliano, Lori. "Ideas for Library Related Assignments." University of Puget Sound, WA. http://library.ups.edu/instruct/assign.htm.

Roberts, Ethel Francine Plusquellic. "Faculty Perceptions of Baccalaureate Nursing Students' Unethical Behavior and the Implications for the Curriculum and Profession." Ph.D. diss., George Mason University, VA, 1996.

Rockman, Ilene F. "The Importance of Assessment." *Reference Services Review* 30, no. 3 (2002): 18.

Rockman, Ilene, and Gordon Smith. "National Higher Education Information and Communication Technology (ICT) Initiative: A Unique Partnership." http://www.calstate.edu/LS/ CARL.ppt.

Rockman, Ilene, Gordon Smith, and Irvin R. Katz. "An Overview of the Higher Education ICT Literacy Assessment." Presentation at the American Library Association's Annual Conference, Chicago, June 23–29, 2005.

Roig, Miguel. "Can Undergraduate Students Determine Whether Text Has Been Plagiarized?" *Psychological Record* 47, no. 1 (1997): 113–22.

Romary, Michael, and Reference Department, Albin O. Kuhn Library & Gallery, University of Maryland, Baltimore County. "Minimum Technological Competencies for Incoming Students at UMBC 2002." Working paper, 2002.

Scanlon, Patrick M., and David R. Neumann. "Internet Plagiarism among College Students." *Journal of College Student Development* 43 (2002): 374–85.

Shapiro, Jeremy J., and Shelley K. Hughes. "Information Literacy as a Liberal Art." *Educom Review* 31, no. 2 (1996): 31–35.

Smith, Kenneth R. "New Roles and Responsibilities for the University Library: Advancing Student Learning through Outcomes Assessment." *ARL*, no. 213 (December 2000): 2.

SupportFreak.com. "Knowledge Base: What Is Oracle?" http://www.mysupport freaks.com/cgi-bin/wsmkb.cgi?SHOW+22+Databases%7COracle#tops.

Svinicki, M. D., and B. A. Schwartz. *Designing Instruction for Library Users: A Practical Guide.* New York: M. Dekker, 1988.

Swanson, Judy. "CSU Information Competence: Please Select a Tutorial . . . Define the Research Topic." California Polytechnic State University, San Luis Obispo. http://www.lib.calpoly.edu/infocomp/modules/.

Thistlethwaite, Polly, Michelle Mach, Kevin Cullen, Lori Oling, Tim Holt, Dennis Ogg, Teresa Y. Neely, and Liz Snyder. "The Data Game." Colorado State University. http://manta.colostate.edu/datagame/.

Toomer, Clarence. "Adult Learner Perceptions of Bibliographic Instructional Services in Five Private Four-Year Liberal Arts Colleges in North Carolina." Ed.D. diss., North Carolina State University, 1993.

UCLA Instructional Services Advisory Committee. "Instructional Competencies Survey Project, 1997–1998." http://www.bol.ucla.edu/%7Ejherschm/project/presentation.htm.

UMBC Information Literacy Task Force. "UMBC Information Literacy Survey—2003 Executive Summary." Albin O. Kuhn Library & Gallery, University of Maryland, Baltimore County. http://aok.lib.umbc.edu/reference/information literacy/ESinfolit2003.pdf.

Universities of Maryland Collaborative. "Universities of Maryland Collaborative Information Literacy Grant Proposal." Working paper, 2004.

University of Maryland University College, Center for Intellectual Property and Copyright. "Faculty and Administrator Perceptions of Academic Integrity: A Survey." 2003. http://www.umuc.edu/distance/odell/cip/research.html.

U.S. Congress. USA PATRIOT Act. Public Law 107-56. 107th Congress. (October 26, 2001).

U.S. Department of Commerce, National Telecommunications and Information Administration. "Falling through the Net: Defining the Digital Divide." 1999. http://www.ntia.doc.gov/ntiahome/fttn99/contents.html.

W3Schools. "ASP Tutorial: Introduction to ASP." http://www.w3schools.com/asp/asp_intro.asp.

Ward, D. A., and W. L. Beck. "Gender and Dishonesty." *Journal of Social Psychology* 130, no. 3 (1990): 333–39.

Ward, D. A., and J. Nantel. "Deterrence or Labeling: The Effect of Informal Sanctions." *Deviant Behavior: An Inter Disciplinary Journal* 14 (1993): 43–64.

Ward, Jonah Allen. "University Students' Views regarding Academic Dishonesty in Two Disciplines." Ph.D. diss., University of Miami, 1998.

WordIQ.com. "DHMO." http://wordiq.com/definition/DHMO.

Wright, Vivian. "The C©pyrightsite." College of Education, University of Alabama. http://www.thecopyrightsite.org/.

INDEX

ABOUT THE AUTHORS

Teresa Y. Neely is Director of the Zimmerman Library, University of New Mexico. Most recently she was Head of Reference at the Albin O. Kuhn Library & Gallery, University of Maryland, Baltimore County, and an Adjunct Professor at the College of Information Studies, University of Maryland, College Park. Neely holds a bachelor of science degree in accounting from South Carolina State College (now University) and received her M.L.S. and Ph.D. degrees (library and information science) from the School of Information Sciences, University of Pittsburgh.

OTHER CONTRIBUTORS

Jessame Ferguson has been the Head of Circulation and Media at the Albin O. Kuhn Library & Gallery, University of Maryland, Baltimore County, since 2002 and Acting Head of Reference and Instruction since 2005. Previously she was the Librarian for Digital Initiatives and Research and Instructional Services Planning at the University of Massachusetts at Amherst, where she helped lead efforts to enhance research experiences for library users at a distance, particularly in online environments. She received her library degree from Louisiana State University.

Olga François teaches information literacy curriculum in the School of Undergraduate Studies at University of Maryland University College and serves as the Senior Research Librarian in the Center for Intellectual Property at UMUC. She received a bachelor's degree in fine arts from Smith College in Northampton, Massachusetts, and an M.L.S. degree from the School of Information Sciences, University of Pittsburgh.

Simmona E. Simmons-Hodo is Services Development and Special Projects Librarian at the Albin O. Kuhn Library & Gallery, University of Maryland, Baltimore County. She also holds a position as Adjunct Professor at the College of Information Sciences at the University of Maryland, College Park. Her selected publications include the forthcoming *Dictionary of Black Architects* (associate editor), *Handbook of Black Librarianship* (contributor), *Writers of Multicultural Fiction: A Bio-Critical Sourcebook* (contributor), and several other articles and research guides. She holds M.L.S. and M.A. degrees from the University of Maryland, College Park.

Katy Sullivan is a Reference and Instruction Librarian at the Albin O. Kuhn Library & Gallery, University of Maryland, Baltimore County. Prior to this position she worked as a Reference Librarian at the Albert S. Cook Library, Towson University. She holds a B.A. in history from Grove City College, Pennsylvania, and an M.L.S. degree from the University of Maryland, College Park.